GETTING BY
IN
JAPANESE

**A quick beginners' course for
tourists and businesspeople**

by Makiko Haruna

BARRON'S

New York/London/Toronto/Sydney

All inquiries should be addressed to:
Barron's Educational Series, Inc.
250 Wireless Boulevard
Hauppauge, New York 11788

International Standard Book No. 0-8120-2664-0

PRINTED IN USA

9   550   987654

Contents

HOKKAIDOO

Sapporo

Aomori

Akita

Sendai

JAPAN SEA

Niigata

HONSHUU Tookyoo

Yokohama

Kyooto Nagoya
Koobe
Hiroshima Oosaka
Nara

Fukuoka SHIKOKU

Nagasaki KYUUSHUU

Kagoshima

PACIFIC OCEAN

OKINAWA

Naha

Note: Doubled vowels indicate long vowels.

4 yon (shi)

The course...and how to use it

Getting by in Japanese

is a five-program course for anyone planning a visit to Japan. It provides a basic survival kit for some of the situations typical of a visit abroad.

The programs

□ concentrate on the language you'll need for "getting by" in common situations—buying food and drink, shopping, finding somewhere to stay, traveling, asking directions, and so on.

□ include real-life conversations recorded by native Japanese speakers.

□ encourage you to develop a good accent by giving you an opportunity to repeat new words and phrases.

□ suggest shortcuts to learning what you need to say and ways of getting the gist of what's being said even if you don't understand every word.

The book includes

□ a short outline of Japanese, and the key words and phrases of each program.

□ the texts of the recorded conversations in the order they are presented in the program.

□ simple grammatical explanations for deeper understanding of Japanese language structure.

□ background information about Japan and Japanese customs.

□ self-checking exercises for you to do between programs, and a short test on the overall course.

□ a reference section containing numbers, days of the week and the month, months of the year, useful addresses, panic situations, the key to the exercises and the test, and a word list.

The two cassettes

contain five programs in dialogue form and allow you to study at your own pace.

To make the most of the course

□ Get accustomed to the sounds of the language by listening to the program without referring to the book.

□ Take every opportunity of repeating aloud what you are asked to say, and concentrate on listening for key words.

□ After each program, work through the explanations and exercises, and if possible practice the conversations with a friend.

□ When you go to Japan, take this book with you, plus a good pocket dictionary and a notebook, so you can jot down the things you discover for yourself.

Outline of the Japanese language

Japanese differs greatly from English in several ways. The following are some of the characteristics of Japanese.

Pronunciation guide

Syllables
Japanese syllables end in vowels or in a nasal *n*. There are no consonant clusters such as *str* of *street* in English. Therefore, *street* is pronounced as **sutoriito**.

Vowels
There are five vowels.

a	like a in *far*	**akai** (red)
e	like e in *pet*	**eki** (station)
i	like ea in *each*	**ikura** (how much)
o	like o in *so*	**osoi** (slow, late)
u	like u in *blue*	**uta** (song)

Length or duration of vowels plays an important role in Japanese, since two words may differ only in length of vowels, such as **kuuki** (air) and **kuki** (stem). Long vowels are roughly twice as long as short vowels and are represented in this book by repeating short vowels. You may also see, on transliterated signs and similar public notices, long vowels indicated by a macron, or line, over the long vowel, e.g., *Kyōto*. Vowels *i* and *u*, when unaccented, tend to be devoiced after a voiceless sound or between two voiceless sounds.

Semi-vowels

There are two semi-vowels: *y* and *w*. They cannot stand as syllables by themselves. A combination of a consonant and a semi-vowel and a vowel may stand as a syllable like **kya**, which sounds like *ca* in English *cat*. Or, a semi-vowel and a vowel may consist of a syllable like **wa**, which sounds like *wo* in *won*.

Consonants

There are 14 consonants, and most of them are found in English. The only two you really have to be careful to pronounce are the following sounds, which are peculiar to Japanese, even though the English alphabet is used in transliteration.

f This sound is different from the English *f* sound. When you pronounce it, your lips come close to

each other, but your teeth do not touch your lower lip. This sound appears only followed by *u* as in **Fujisan** (Mt. Fuji).

r This is neither English *r* nor *l*, but has a sound between those English sounds. You need not be too nervous about these sounds, since *r* and *l* do not contrast in Japanese.

Double consonants like *tt* in **kitte** (postage stamp) are said with a one-syllable pause between the preceding and the following syllable—**kit te**.

N is often pronounced like *m* when it is followed by a *p*, *b*, or *m* sound.

Accent

Unlike English, Japanese has a pitch accent. Accented syllables are given a higher pitch in Japanese, whereas they are louder in English. Japanese dialects often vary in accent patterns.

Writing

Three different types of script are used in writing Japanese: *hiragana*, *katakana*, and *kanji* (Chinese characters). Each symbol of *hiragana* and *katakana* stands for a sound, or more precisely a syllable; *kanji* express meaning. *Katakana* is used to write borrowed words like **koohii** (coffee) and **nyuusu** (news), as well as foreign names like **Amerika** (America) and **Bobu** (Bob).

Japanese may be written vertically or horizontally. When it is written vertically from top to bottom, lines proceed from right to left. When it is written horizontally, lines proceeded from left to right, as in English.

Transliteration is used in this book. Certain words, however, are written in characters as well as in transliteration, since it will be very useful for you to be able to recognize those words written in Japanese.

Structure

Word order is relatively free in Japanese, though a predicate verb or adjective normally ends the sentence.

A particle following a noun specifies some relation between the noun and a predicate verb or adjective. For instance, **wa** marks the topic of a sentence, **ga** the grammatical subject, **o** the object, **ni** the dative, **no** the genitive. Some particles may be dropped in spoken Japanese as long as ambiguity does not result.

Word order does not change in interrogative sentences. When forming questions, put **ka** at the end of the sentence and, if necessary, use a question word like **nani** (what), **itsu** (when), **doko** (where).

Understood elements can be dropped in Japanese. You may even drop subjects or objects when you are sure the listener can understand what you are saying.

Singular and plural

There is no clear distinction in Japanese between singular and plural nouns. Plural nouns are not usually expressed formally, although there are a few plural suffixes, such as -**tachi**, which optionally follow nouns referring to people, like man, woman, child, or teacher.

Gender and articles

Japanese has neither gender (masculine, feminine, neuter) nor articles (a, an, the).

Levels of speech

There are basically two levels of politeness in speech, formal and informal. Conversations in this book are written in the polite or formal level. Most people who speak to you—shopkeepers, clerks, receptionists, waitresses—will use the formal speech. Though you might have a choice between formal and informal speech, nobody will be offended if you use polite speech. Generally speaking, women's speech tends to be more polite than men's speech.

Some nouns may be prefixed in polite speech by **o** or **go**—for example, **kanjoo/okanjoo** (bill) and **hon/gohon** (book). These prefixes are put in parens when either form is equally acceptable.

(Doomo) arigatoo (thank you [very much]), for instance, has corresponding more polite forms **(doomo) arigatoo gozaimasu** (thank you [very much] for what you are going to do or have just done for me) and **(doomo) arigatoo gozaimashita** (thank you [very much] for what you did for me).

Honorific forms vs. humble forms

There are two ways to express respect toward the listener or another person in a sentence. Since respect can be expressed by the relative positions of the two persons in question, the speaker either "elevates" the person or "lowers" himself.

The speaker uses honorific forms to "elevate" the person. The honorific prefix **o-** or **go-** precedes nouns referring to the person or a thing related to that person. For example, **namae** (name) takes **o-** in the honorific form: **onamae**. Verbs also have honorific forms. A polite imperative, **matte kudasai** (please wait), for instance, becomes **o-machi kudasai** in the honorific form.

The most important thing to remember is that you can never use an honorific form to refer to yourself, members of your family or group, or a thing related to you or to members of your family or group. When honorific forms or expressions appear in this book, a note is attached to remind you of this point.

Humble forms are used by the speaker to "lower" himself, so that he can relatively "elevate" the other person. The speaker uses humble forms to refer to himself, or to members of his family or group.

1 Ordering and paying

Key words

A coffee, please.	**Koohii o onegai-shimasu.**
The bill, please.	**Okanjoo o onegai-shimasu.**
Two coffees and one tea, please.	**Koohii o futatsu to koocha o hitotsu onegai-shimasu.**
What do you have?	**Nani ga arimasu ka?**
Excuse me.	**Sumimasen.**
Thank you.	**Arigatoo.**
Yes	**Hai.**
No	**Iie.**
0, 1, 2, 3,	**zero/rei, ichi, ni, san,**
4, 5, 6,	**shi/yon, go, roku,**
7, 8, 9,	**shichi/nana, hachi, ku/kyuu,**
10	**juu**
1, 2, 3,	**hitotsu, futatsu, mittsu,**
4, 5, 6,	**yottsu, itsutsu, muttsu,**
7, 8, 9,	**nanatsu, yattsu, kokonotsu,**
10	**too**

Conversations

These conversations can be heard on the cassettes. New words can be found in the Japanese–English word list (p. 71).

Ordering a coffee

Waitress   Irasshaimase.
Customer   Koohii o onegai-shimasu.
Waitress   Hai, kashikomarimashita.

irasshaimase *welcome*
kashikomarimashita *certainly, sir.*

Ordering a tea

Waitress	Irasshaimase.
Customer	Koocha o onegai-shimasu.
Waitress	Remon-tii desu ka, miruku-tii desu ka?
Customer	Remon-tii o onegai-shimasu.
Waitress	Hai, wakarimashita.

Remon-tii desu ka, miruku-tii desu ka? *(Which will you have) tea with lemon or tea with cream?*
wakarimashita *(I) understood*

Ordering two coffees

Waiter	Irasshaimase.
Customer	Koohii o futatsu onegai-shimasu.
Waiter	Hai, kashikomarimashita.

Ordering three cokes and one orange juice

Waitress	Irasshaimase.
Customer	Koora o mittsu to orenji-juusu o hitotsu onegai-shimasu.
Waitress	Hai, wakarimashita.

to *and* (to connects nouns but not sentences)

Ordering two bottles of beer and one white wine

Waiter	Irasshaimase.
Customer	Biiru wa nani ga arimasu ka?
Waiter	Asahi to Kirin to Sapporo ga arimasu.
Customer	Jaa, Asahi o ni-hon to wain o ip-pai onegai-shimasu.
Waiter	Wain wa aka desu ka, shiro desu ka?
Customer	Shiro-wain o onegai-shimasu.
Waiter	Hai, kashikomarimashita.

biiru *beer*
Asahi, Kirin and Sapporo are brand names of beer.
jaa *well, . . .*
-hon; -pai *counter suffixes (see p. 15)*
wain *wine*
aka *red*
shiro *white*

Paying the bill

Customer   Sumimasen. Okanjoo o onegai-shimasu.

Waiter   Hai, kashikomarimashita. Shooshoo o-machi-kudasai.

Waiter   (handing the bill to the customer) Hai, doozo. Doomo arigatoo gozaimashita.

Shooshoo o-machi-kudasai *Please wait a moment*
Hai, doozo *Here it is*

Explanations

Counting

Japanese has two sets of numerals: the native Japanese numerals (hito-, futa-, mi-, . . .) and numerals of Chinese origin (ichi, ni, san, . . .). The latter can express numbers in the abstract, and can also be used in counting things, though they have to be followed by counter suffixes suitable for what is being counted. Some of these counter suffixes are as follows:

-mai   for thin, flat objects (paper, shirts, stamps)
-nin   for people (except for **hitori**, one person, and **futari**, two people)
-hon   for long, slender objects (bottles of beer, pencils, trees)
-hai   for cups or glasses of liquid

(Note: The **h** of **hon** and **hai** changes following certain numbers. It changes to **p** after one, six, ten, and optionally eight, while those root numbers are contracted. It changes to **b** after three.)

		-hon	-hai
1	ichi	ip-pon	ip-pai
6	roku	rop-pon	rop-pai
8	hachi	hap-pon	hap-pai
		hachi-hon	hachi-hai
10	juu	jup-pon	jup-pai

For the number 3, the *h* changes to *b*.

3	san	san-bon	san-bai

Counter suffixes also follow the question word **nan** (what) to create the question "how many" (**nan-nin**, **nan-mai**). The **h** sound of -**hon** and -**hai** changes to **b** in **nan-bon** and **nan-bai**.

The native Japanese numerals only go up to 10. Followed by the suffix -**tsu** (**hitotsu, futatsu, mittsu**), they can be used to count solid things (apples, stones, cakes) and also abstract things (problems, ideas, orders at coffee shops and restaurants). **Ikutsu** is the question word for "how many" or "how much" used when asking about items counted this way.

Particle *wa*

Wa introduces the topic of a sentence; the rest of the sentence is the comment on the topic. The topic normally occupies the beginning of the sentence.

Keeki wa nani ga
arimasu ka?

*As for pastry, what
do you have?*

Wain wa aka o onegai-
shimasu.

As for wine, red, please.

Particle *ga*

Ga indicates the grammatical subject of a sentence.

Nani ga arimasu ka?

*What exists? What do
you have?*

Yama ga kirei desu.

The mountain is pretty.

Particle *o*

O indicates the grammatical object of a sentence.

Mizu o kudasai.

Give me water, please.

Koohii o nomimasu.

I drink coffee.

Exercises

1 Order the following items for yourself (see "Drinks and Snacks," page 18).

a Coffee, please. _____

b Red wine, please. _____

c Sapporo brand beer. _____

d Ice cream and coke. _____

e Cake and tea. _____

2 Order the following for your friends and yourself.

a Three coffees, please. _____
b Two teas with lemon, and one coke. _____
c One tea with cream, one tomato juice, and
two orange juice. _____
d One bottle of white wine. _____
e Three bottles of beer and a glass of vodka,
uokka. _____

3 How do you ask what kinds they have of the
following items?

a ice cream _____
b cake _____
c spaghetti _____
d sandwich _____
e dessert, **dezaato** _____

4 There is no menu on your table in a coffee shop.
The waiter doesn't even notice you. How will you get
the waiter's attention and how do you ask for a
menu, **menyuu**?

_____
_____

_____

Worth Knowing

Tipping

In Japan, you need not worry about how much
money you have to leave at a table as a tip. You must
pay service charge and tax, however, when you eat
or drink in a hotel or when the cost of food and drink
per person exceeds a certain amount. When they
must be paid, they are included in the bill. All you
have to pay is the total appearing on the bill.

You need not give a tip to a taxi driver, nor to a
cloakroom attendant. However, a tip is often given to
a maid in a Japanese-style inn, since she assists you

in many ways, such as serving you tea and sweets when you arrive in your room, serving dinner and breakfast in your room, and preparing the bedding when you retire for the night.

Japanese liquor

(O)sake or **Nihon-shu** is made from rice and usually served warm in a little bottlelike container called **ochooshi** or **tokkuri**, which is counted by the counter suffix **-hon** (see p. 15). The little cup you drink **sake** from is called **sakazuki**.

(O)sake can also be served cold with ice in a glass.

The term **(o)sake** can also be used to refer to liquor in general. **Nihon-shu** has only one meaning— Japanese rice liquor (what Americans know as **saké**).

Drinks and snacks

water	**mizu**	水
coffee	**koohii**	コーヒー
	(Japanese coffee is thicker than American coffee.)	
	amerikan koohii	
	American coffee	アメリカン・コーヒー
	aisu koohii	
	iced coffee	アイスコーヒー
	uinnaa koohii	
	cafe Viennese	ウィンナー コーヒー
tea	**koocha**	紅 茶
	remon-tii	
	tea with lemon	レモン ティー
	miruku-tii	
	tea with cream	ミルク ティー
	aisu tii	
	iced tea	アイス ティー
Japanese tea	**ocha**	お 茶
	Nihon-cha	日本茶
hot chocolate	**kokoa**	ココア

milk	**miruku**	ミルク
	gyuunyuu	牛乳
	hotto miruku	
	hot milk	ホット ミルク
soft drinks	**koora** *coke*	コーラ
	sooda *soda*	ソーダ
	orenji juusu	
	orange juice	オレンジ ジュース
	tomato juusu	
	tomato juice	トマト ジュース
	remoneedo	
	lemonade	レモネード
	kuriimu-soda	
	ice-cream soda	クリーム ソーダ
beer	**biiru**	ビール
	kuro-biiru	
	dark beer	黒ビール
	nama-biiru	
	draught beer	生ビール
wine	**wain**	ワイン
	aka-wain	
	red wine	赤ワイン
	shiro-wain	
	white wine	白ワイン
rice wine	**(o)sake**	お酒
	Nihon-shu	日本酒
whiskey	**uisukii**	ウィスキー
sugar	**satoo**	砂糖
pastry	**keeki**	ケーキ
ice cream	**aisukuriimu**	アイスクリーム
custard pudding	**purin**	プリン
toast	**toosuto**	トースト
jam	**jamu**	ジャム
	ichigo-jamu	
	strawberry jam	苺ジャム
	maamareedo	
	marmalade	マーマレード
pancakes	**hotto keeki**	ホットケーキ
sandwich	**sandoitchi**	サンドイッチ

	hamu-sando(itchi)	
	ham sandwich	ハムサンド
	tamago-sando(itchi)	
	egg sandwich	卵サンド
	yasai-sando(itchi)	
	vegetable sandwich	野菜サンド
	mikkusu-sando(itchi)	
	mixed sandwich	ミックスサンド
spaghetti	**supagetii**	スパゲティー

Coffee shops and bars

There are many coffee shops, **kissaten**, in Japan.
They serve coffee, tea, soft drinks, ice cream, cakes,
and so on. Many of them serve snacks and light
dishes too, such as sandwiches, spaghetti, pancakes,
and fried rice.

Ladies called **hosutesu** (hostesses) work at bars and
they converse with customers over a drink. You have
to pay for the drinks the **hosutesu** have had with you
as well as the drinks you had. If you do not like this
arrangement, you can enjoy drinks at bars in hotels
without **hosutesu** being with you.

Using "excuse me"

Sumimasen or **doomo sumimasen** (excuse me; I
am very sorry) has several uses besides expressing
apology. When you want to attract someone's
attention, you can say **sumimasen**. For instance, you
can call a waiter or waitress at a coffee shop or
restaurant by saying **sumimasen**. You may begin
conversations with it when you want to ask a person
whom you do not know for directions or information.

Gratitude can also be expressed by **(doomo)
sumimasen** (thank you very much, but you shouldn't
have done it). Japanese people tend to express an
apology first for having caused someone
inconvenience.

2 Shopping

Key words

How much is it?	**Ikura desu ka?**
Give me this one, please.	**Kore o kudasai.**
That one, 100 grams, please.	**Sore o hyaku-guramu kudasai.**
Two 50-yen stamps, please.	**Go-juu-en-kitte o ni-mai kudasai.**
Show me that one, please.	**Are o misete-kudasai.**
Show me a bigger one.	**Motto ookii no o misete-kudasai.**
By airmail, please.	**Kookuubin de onegai-shimasu.**
Fill it up with gas, please.	**Mantan ni shite-kudasai.**
Exchange this for yen, please.	**En ni kaete-kudasai.**
20, 30, 40, . . .	**ni-juu, san-juu, yon-juu . . .**
100, . . . 300, . . .	**hyaku, . . . san-byaku, . . .**
600, . . .	**rop-pyaku, . . .**
1000, . . . 3000, . . .	**sen, . . . san-zen, . . .**
8000, . . .	**has-sen, . . .**

Conversations

Buying by weight

Shopkeeper Irasshaimase.
Customer Kore o ni-hyaku-guramu kudasai.
Shopkeeper Hai, kashikomarimashita.
Customer Ikura desu ka?
Shopkeeper Rop-pyaku yon-juu en desu.

kore *this* (see p. 24)
desu *is/am/are*

Buying by numbers

Shopkeeper	Irasshaimase.
Customer	Kono (o)manjuu wa ikura desu ka?
Shopkeeper	Hitotsu hyaku go-juu en desu.
Customer	Mittsu kudasai.
Shopkeeper	Doomo arigatoo gozaimasu.

(o)manjuu *Japanese sweet cake*
kono (see p. 25)

Asking the salesperson to show an item

Salesperson	Irasshaimase.
Customer	Sore o misete-kudasai.
Salesperson	Kore desu ka?
Customer	Hai, soo desu.
Salesperson	(handing item to the customer)
Customer	Hai, doozo.

Hai, soo desu *Yes, you are right/that's right*

Finding the correct size

Customer	Emu-saizu o misete-kudasai.
Salesperson	(handing an item to the customer) Hai, doozo. Ikaga desu ka?
Customer	Chotto chiisai desu. Motto ookii no o misete-kudasai.
Salesperson	(handing another item to the customer) Eru-saizu desu. Doozo. Ikaga desu ka?
Customer	Choodo ii desu. Kore wa ikura desu ka?
Salesperson	Go-sen hap-pyaku en desu.
Customer	Jaa, kore o kudasai.
Salesperson	Doomo arigatoo gozaimasu.

emu-saizu *size M*
eru-saizu *size L*
Ikaga desu ka? *How does it fit you/How do you like it?*
chotto *a little*

chiisai *small*
motto *more*
no (see p. 25)
ookii *big*
choodo *just*
ii *good*

Buying stamps and aerograms

Customer   Hyaku-en-kitte o ichi-mai to go-juu en
              kitte o yon-mai kudasai. Sorekara,
              kookuushokan o san-mai kudasai.
Clerk   Hai. Minna de rop-pyaku roku-juu en
              desu.

kookuushokan *aerogram*
sorekara *furthermore*
minna de *in all*

Sending an air mail letter at the post office

Customer	(handing a letter to the clerk) Kore wa ikura desu ka?
Clerk	Kookuubin desu ka, senbin desu ka?
Customer	Kookuubin de onegai-shimasu.
Clerk	Hyaku go-juu en desu.

kookuubin *airmail*
senbin *surface mail*

At the gas station

Customer	Mantan ni shite-kudasai.
Shopkeeper	Hai, kashikomarimashita.

At the bank

Clerk	Irasshaimase.
Customer	En ni kaete-kudasai.
Clerk	Hai, kashikomarimashita.

Explanations

Demonstratives for things

Pointing at a thing is probably the easiest way to make people understand which one you want or mean. In Japanese demonstratives, the pointing words, differ according to the location of the object.

Demonstrative pronouns are used alone:

kore this; an object located near the speaker
sore that; an object located near the listener
are that; an object located relatively far from both speaker and listener
dore which

Adjectival demonstratives are used in conjunction with other nouns:

kono	kono koohii	this coffee
sono	sono kitte	that stamp
ano	ano hito	that person
dono	dono basu	which bus

Substitute no

Another way to specify a thing whose name you need not mention is to use **no** with an adjective of size, color, and so on.

ookii no	big one	chiisai no	small one
akai no	red one	aoi no	blue one
atsui no	hot one	tsumetai no	cold one

No can also be preceded by a personal pronoun or a proper name.

| watashi no | mine | anata no | yours |
| Yamada-san no | Yamada's | Tomu no | Tom's |

Polite imperative

Kudasai means "give me, please" by itself.

| Are o kudasai. | Give me that one, please. |
| Koohii o kudasai. | A coffee, please. |

You can use **kudasai**, too, in the place of **onegai-shimasu**, which we used in Program 1, in ordering things at a coffee shop, a restaurant, or a bar, though there exists a subtle difference in meaning between the two expressions. **Kudasai** is a more direct request; **onegai-shimasu** has a wider range of meaning that makes a request more modest.

Kudasai when combined with a certain form of verb, the **-te** form, expresses the polite imperative. You can use this construction when you want to ask someone to do something for you. The following are some polite imperative forms you may use.

| misete-kudasai | please show me |
| kite-kudasai | please come |

matte-kudasai	please wait
michi o oshiete-kudasai	please show me the way
mado o shimete-kudasai	please close the window
doa o akete-kudasai	please open the door

Particle *de*

De indicates a means, way, or method.

Senbin de onegai-shimasu.	By surface mail, please.
Kono densha de ikimasu.	I go by this train.
(O)hashi de tabemasu.	We eat with chopsticks.

Numbers

10	**juu**	100	**hyaku**	1000	**sen**
20	**ni-juu**	200	**ni-hyaku**	2000	**ni-sen**
30	**san-juu**	300	**san-byaku**	3000	**san-zen**
40	**yon-juu**	400	**yon-hyaku**	4000	**yon-sen**
50	**go-juu**	500	**go-hyaku**	5000	**go-sen**
60	**roku-juu**	600	**rop-pyaku**	6000	**roku-sen**
70	**nana-juu**	700	**nana-hyaku**	7000	**nana-sen**
80	**hachi-juu**	800	**hap-pyaku**	8000	**has-sen**
90	**kyuu-juu**	900	**kyuu-hyaku**	9000	**kyuu-sen**

(**-hyaku** becomes **-byaku** after 3 and **-pyaku** after 6 and 8; **-sen** becomes **-zen** after 3; see p. 15)

Exercises

---

1 Say the following numbers in Japanese.

150, 260, 370, 410, 1600, 3520, 4090, 5700, 8880.

2 Buy the following things.

a two bottles of Japanese rice wine
b 300 grams of ham, **hamu**
c four grapefruit, **gureepufuruutsu**
d two 500-yen stamps
e ten aerograms

3 Ask the salesperson to show the following items (see "Color, size and degree terms" on page 29).

a the one near the salesperson
b the one on the shelf over there
c the red one
d the black one
e the blue one
f a smaller one
g a lighter one
h a cheaper one

4 Complete the following conversation at a shoe department.

Salesperson	Irasshaimase.
You	(you want to see the shoes over there)

_____

Salesperson	Saizu wa?
You	(suppose your shoe size is 28 cm. (**senchi(meetoru)**, cm.)_____

_____

Salesperson	Ikaga desu ka?
You	(they are a little too small; say so) ____

_____

You	(ask to see bigger ones) _____

_____

You	(ask the salesperson how much they are)_____

_____

5 Say in Japanese

a Surface mail, please_____
b How much is this by airmail? _____
c Please change into dollars _____

Worth knowing

Metric system

The metric system is used in measuring length, weight, volume, and temperature in Japan.

Important metric unit words

gram (g)	**guramu**
kilogram (kg)	**kiro(guramu)**
liter (l)	**rittoru**
centimeter (cm)	**senchi(meetoru)**
meter (m)	**meetoru**
kilometer (km)	**kiro(meetoru)**
— °C	**(sesshi) — °do**
— °F	**kashi — °do**

Metric equivalents

Metric	*= English*	*English*	*= Metric*
1 kg	= 2.2 lb	1 lb	= 450 g
1 l	= 0.26 gal (U.S.)	1 gal	= 4.5 l
1 cm	= 0.39 in	1 in	= 2.5 cm
1 m	= 3.3 ft	1 ft	= 30 cm
1 km	= 0.62 mile	1 mile	= 1.6 km
0°C	= 32°F		
37°C	= 98.6°F		
100°C	= 212°F		

Names of stores and facilities

department store	**depaato**	デパート
	hyakkaten	百貨店
-department	**-uriba**	売 場
supermarket	**suupaa**	スーパー
bookstore	**hon-ya**	本 屋
bakery	**pan-ya**	パン屋
drugstore	**kusuri-ya**	薬 屋
meat market	**niku-ya**	肉 屋
green grocer	**yao-ya**	八百屋
fish market	**sakana-ya**	魚 屋
candy and snack shop	**(o)kashi-ya**	お菓子屋
gas station	**gasorin sutando**	ガソリン スタンド
post office	**yuubinkyoku**	郵便局
bank	**ginkoo**	銀 行
restaurant	**resutoran**	レストラン

Color, size and degree terms (adjectives)

red	**akai**	white	**shiroi**
blue	**aoi**	black	**kuroi**
green	**aoi**	yellow	**kiiroi**
heavy	**omoi**	light	**karui**
big	**ookii**	small	**chiisai**
long	**nagai**	short	**mijikai**
high	**takai**	low	**hikui**
expensive	**takai**	cheap	**yasui**
hot	**atsui**	cold (food,	**tsumetai**
salty; hot	**karai**	drink)	
sweet	**amai**	cold	**samui**
bitter (taste)	**nigai**	(weather)	

Japanese currency

Japanese currency is **en**. Coins are 1 en, 5 en, 10 en, 50 en, 100 en and 500 en. Notes are 1000 en, 5000 en, and 10,000 en.

Foreign currency

dollar	**doru**
pound	**pondo**
mark	**maruku**

3 Traveling

Key words

Where is the ticket booth?	**Kippu-uriba wa doko desu ka?**
Two adult tickets to Nara.	**Nara made otona ni-mai.**
To Kyooto Station, please.	**Kyooto-eki e itte kudasai.**
What is the way to Kobe?	**Koobe wa doo ittara, ii desu ka?**
Hikari leaving at 3:00 p.m.	**gogo san-ji hatsu no Hikari**
A bus for Tokyo station	**Tookyoo-eki iki no basu**
11, 12, . . . 99	**juu-ichi, juu-ni, . . . kyuu-juu-kyuu**
1st, 2nd, 3rd, . . .	**hitotsu-me, futatsu-me, mittsu-me, . . .**

Conversations

Where is the ticket booth?

Tourist	Sumimasen. Kippu-uriba wa doko desu ka?
Passerby	Asoko desu.
Tourist	Doomo arigatoo.
Passerby	Doo itashimashite.

kippu *ticket*
uriba *selling place*
doko *where*
asoko *over there* (see p. 32)
doo itashimashite *never mind, you're welcome*

Where is the bus stop?

Tourist	Sumimasen. Yokohama-eki-iki no basu no noriba wa doko desu ka?

Passerby	Ano kado o hidari ni magatta tokoro desu.
Tourist	Doomo arigatoo gozaimashita.
Passerby	Doo itashimashite.

noriba *place for boarding a vehicle*
kado *corner*
hidari *left*
magatta tokooro desu *the place is after the turn*

How can I get to/go to Kinkaku-ji?

Tourist	Kinkaku-ji wa doo ittara, ii desu ka?
Passerby	Kono michi o massugu itte, futatsu-me no shingoo o migi ni magatta tokoro desu.
Tourist	Hai, wakarimashita. Doomo arigatoo gozaimashita.
Passerby	Doo itashimashite.

doo *how*
ittara *if (you) go*
michi *road, street*
massugu *straight*
itte, . . . *(you) go and . . .*
shingoo *traffic signal*
migi *right*

How can I go to Kobe?

Tourist	Sumimasen. Koobe wa doo ittara, ii desu ka?
Passerby	Kono densha de Nishinomiya made itte, Nishinomiya de Koobe-iki no densha ni norikaete kudasai.
Tourist	Hai, wakarimashita. Doomo arigatoo.
Passerby	Doo itashimashite.

densha *train*
made *as far as*
norikaemasu *to change a train, bus*

Buying Tickets to Tokyo

Tourist   Tookyoo made, otóna san-mai, kodomo ni-mai.

Clerk   Rop-pyaku hachi-juu en desu.

otona *adult*
kodomo *child*

Buying a Hikari ticket in advance

Tourist   Juu-ichi-gatsu mikka, gozen ku-ji-hatsu no Hikari no kippu, Kyooto made.

Clerk   Nan-mai desu ka?

Tourist   Ichi-mai.

-gatsu *a month of the year*
juu-ichi gatsu *November*
mikka *third day of the month*
gozen *a.m.*
-ji *o'clock*
-hatsu *(departure time)*
Hikari *the name of a train*

In a taxi

Tourist   Tookyoo-eki e itte kudasai.

Driver   Hai.

When you are asked the way

Passerby   Sumimasen. Toire wa doko desu ka?

Foreigner   Sumimasen. Shirimasen.

toire *toilet*
shirimasen *not know*

Explanations

Demonstratives for place

The place in question may be shown by pointing. The relationship between a place and its distance from the

speaker or the listener is the same as that between a thing and its location, discussed on page 24.

koko	here
soko	there
asoko	over there
doko	where

Particles: *o, ni, e, made, no, de*

O indicates the place where one performs a motion like walking, running, flying, turning, crossing.

Kono michi o massugu itte kudasai.	Please go straight along this road.
Ano kado o magatte kudasai.	Please turn at that corner.

Ni and **e** indicate direction.

Migi ni/e magatte kudasai.	Please turn to the right.
Nara ni/e ikimasu.	I go to Nara.

Made indicates a time or distance limit.

Yokohama made ikimasu.	I go as far as Yokohama.
Roku-ji made nemasu.	I sleep until 6 o'clock.

No follows a noun when it modifies another noun.

Tookyoo-eki-iki no basu no noriba	a bus stop for the bus for Tokyo Station
Hikari no kippu	a Hikari ticket

De indicates the place where an action is performed.

Kyooto de norikaete-kudasai.	Please change at Kyoto.
Depaato de kaimasu.	I'll buy it at a department store.

Months of the year: See page 66.

Days of the month: See page 66.

Numbers

11	juu-ichi	12	juu-ni
21	ni-juu-ichi	23	ni-juu-san
31	san-juu-ichi	34	san-juu-shi/yon
41	yon-juu-ichi	45	yon-juu-go
51	go-juu-ichi	56	go-juu-roku
61	roku-juu-ichi	67	roku-juu-nana/shichi
71	nana-juu-ichi	78	nana-juu-hachi
81	hachi-juu-ichi	89	hachi-juu-ku
91	kyuu-juu-ichi	92	kyuu-juu-ni

Ordinal numbers

Ordinal numbers (first, second, third) can be formed by attaching -**me** to the counting numerals of **hitotsu**, **futatsu**, **mittsu**, and so on, or to units of numerals and counter suffixes.

futatsu-me no shingoo   the second signal
san-bon-me no biiru   the third bottle of beer

Or, -**ban-me** is attached directly to numerals of Chinese origin: **ichi-ban-me**, **ni-ban-me**, **san-ban-me**.

Time (1)

-**Ji** indicates the hour.

san-ji   3 o'clock   **juu-ni-ji**   12 o'clock

Half-past the hour is expressed by inserting **han** after the -**ji**.

go-ji-han   5:30   **ku-ji-han**   9:30

Gozen means morning, and **gogo** afternoon. They are used to indicate **a.m.** and **p.m.** and they come before the time.

gozen shichi-ji   7:00 a.m.
gogo roku-ji han   6:30 p.m.

Exercises

1 Buy train tickets

a two adults and two children to Osaka
b one adult and three children to Sendai
c four adults and six children to Kamakura
d five adults and one child to Nara
e one adult and one child to Kyoto by Kodama
   leaving at 3 o'clock

2 Ask the location of the following and find them on
the map on pages 38–39.

a taxi station
   You   _____
   Passerby Asoko desu.

b toilet (**toire** or **otearai**)
   You   _____
   Passerby Eki no naka desu. (**naka** inside)

c post office
   You   _____
   Passerby Kono michi o massugu itte, mittsu-me no
               kado no tokoro desu.

d bank
   You   _____
   Passerby Kono michi o massugu itte, futatsu-me no
               shingoo o hidari ni magatte, hyaku-
               meetoru gurai itta tokoro desu.
               (**gurai** approximate amount)

e bus stop for the bus for Sagano
   You   _____
   Passerby Ano kado o hidari ni magatta tokoro desu.

3 Ask the way to the following places and find them
on the map.

a Yasaka-jinja (**jinja**, shrine)
   You   _____
   Passerby Kono michi o massugu itte, futatsu-

me no shingoo o migi ni magatte, hitotsu-me no kado o hidari ni magatta tokoro desu.

b Arashiyama
You _____
Passerby Kono densha de Katsura made itte, Katsura de Arashiyama-iki no densha ni norikaete-kudasai.

Worth knowing

Transportation fares

Children under six years of age ride free on public transportation, such as buses, trains, and subways. Fares for children ages six through eleven are approximately half those for adults.

If you are going to use the same line many times, you'd be better off buying a book of tickets, **kaisuu-ken**, with about a 10 percent discount. You can buy a Japan Rail Pass in the U.S.A. and use it as often as you want when you ride Japan National Railway trains. One-week, two-week, and three-week passes are available.

Vending machines for train and subway tickets

Tickets are sold by vending machines at many stations in big cities. You can use bills in some machines, but many machines take only coins. There should be at least one ticket booth open at which a clerk sells tickets, even at an almost fully automated station.

Fares are progressive in Japan, just like those in Washington D.C. or San Francisco. The cost of your ride depends on how far you go. After consulting the maps above or on the vending machines, you can purchase a ticket for the proper fare.

Super express trains

The special lines on which only super express trains run are called **shinkansen**. Two types of trains, limited expresses and ordinary expresses, are operated on each line. For instance, the **Hikari** stops only at some stations between Tokyo and Hakata on the **Tokaido-shinkansen** line, while the **Kodama** stops at all stations.

So far, there are three **shinkansen**. The **Tokaido shinkansen** runs between Tokyo and Hakata on Kyushu (7 hours and 36 minutes by **Hikari**). The **Tohoku shinkansen** runs between Omiya and Morioka (3 hours and 17 minutes by **Yamabiko**). The **Joetsu shinkansen** runs between Omiya and Niigata (1 hour and 45 minutes by **Asahi**).

Some seats are reserved and others are not. The first-class coaches are called **guriin-sha** (green coach).

Names of facilities

(o)tera	temple	お　寺
jinja	shrine	神　社
kyookai	church	教　会
taishikan	embassy	大使館
Amerika Taishikan	American embassy	アメリカ大使館
ryoojikan	consulate general	領事館
byooin	hospital	病　院
biyooin	beauty salon	美容院
keisatsu	police	警　察
hakubutsukan	museum	博物館
bijutsukan	art museum	美術館
doobutsuen	zoo	動物園
shokubutsuen	botanical garden	植物園
kooen	park	公　園
teien	garden	庭　園
eiga-kan	movie theater	映画館
gekijoo	theater	劇　場
annai-sho	information center; information desk	案内所
eki	station	駅
chikatetsu	subway	地下鉄

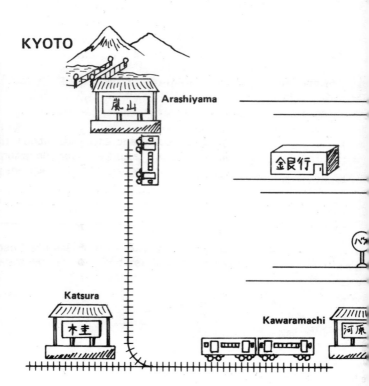

KYOTO

Arashiyama 嵐山

金艮行

Katsura 木圭

Kawaramachi 河原

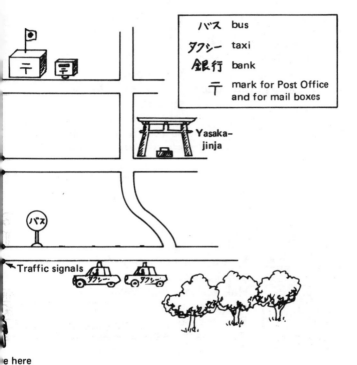

バス	bus
タクシー	taxi
銀行	bank
〒	mark for Post Office and for mail boxes

Yasaka-jinja

バス

Traffic signals

タクシー タクシー

e here

4 Telephone conversations

Key words

Hello	**Moshi moshi**
Please reserve (seats) at 8:00.	**Hachi-ji ni yoyaku o onegai-shimasu.**
Do you have a (vacant) room tonight?	**Konban heya ga arimasu ka?**
A party of two.	**Futari desu.**
May I speak to Mr. Sato?	**Satoo-san o onegai-shimasu.**
10,000 20,000	**ichi-man, ni-man,**
30,000 40,000	**san-man, you-man**
90,000 100,000	**kyuu-man, juu-man**

Conversations

Making a reservation at a restaurant

Tourist   Moshi moshi, Fuji-resutoran desu ka?

Manager   Hai, soo desu.

Tourist   Konban hachi-ji juu-go-fun ni yo-nin yoyaku o onegai-shimasu.

Manager   Hai, kashikomarimashita. (O)namae o onegai-shimasu.

Tourist   Brown desu.

Manager   Buraun-san desu ne. Dewa, hachi-ji juu-go-fun ni o-machi-shite imasu. Arigatoo gozaimashita.

konban   *tonight*
-fun   *(indicates the minute)*
-nin   *counter suffix for persons* (see p. 15)
(o)namae   *name (onamae is honorific, so never use it to refer to your own name)*
-san   *Mr., Mrs., Miss* (see p. 44)
dewa   *well,*
o-machi-shite-imasu   *we are waiting for you*

Wrong number

Tourist	Moshi moshi, Resutoran Sakura desu ka?
Woman	Iie, chigaimasu.
Tourist	Doomo sumimasen.

chigaimasu *be wrong, be different*

Finding a place to stay

Tourist	Moshi moshi, Hoteru Kyuushuu desu ka?
Receptionist	Hai, soo desu.
Tourist	Konban heya ga arimasu ka?
Receptionist	Sumimasen ga, konban wa man'in desu.

man'in *full*

Making a reservation at a hotel

Operator	Moshi moshi, Shikoku Hoteru desu.
Tourist	Yoyaku o onegai-shimasu.
Operator	Hai. Shooshoo o-machi-kudasai.
Receptionist	Moshi moshi, yoyaku-gakari desu.
Tourist	Raishuu no getsu-yoobi kara sui-yoobi made, san-paku, heya ga arimasu ka?
Receptionist	Nan-nin desu ka?
Tourist	Futari desu.
Receptionist	Hai, gozaimasu. Tsuin ga ip-paku ichi-man has-sen en de, daburu ga ichi-man go-sen en desu.
Tourist	Daburu o onegai-shimasu.
Receptionist	Hai, kashikomarimashita. (O)namae o onegai-shimasu.

-gakari *a person or section in charge of*
-haku (-paku after the contracted forms of 1, 6, and 10, and 3, 4, and the question word *nan*) *counter suffix for nights to stay*
raishuu *next week*
getsu-yoobi *Monday*
sui-yoobi *Wednesday*
kara *from*
tsuin *a room with twin beds*
daburu *a room with a double bed*

Calling up a friend at the office

Operator	Moshi moshi, Nippon-shooji desu.
Brown	Jinji-ka no Satoo-san o onegai-shimasu.
Operator	Satoo wa yasumi desu.
Brown	Soo desu ka? Satoo-san no ie no denwa-bangoo wa nan-ban desu ka?
Operator	0 (zero) 3 (san) no 5 (go) 8 (hachi) 6 (roku) no 4 (yon) 2 (ni) 1 (ichi) 9 (kyuu) desu.
Brown	Doomo arigatoo gozaimashita.
Operator	Doo itashimashite.

shooji-gaisha *trading company*
jinji-ka *personnel section*
yasumi *absence, day off, vacation*
ie *house, home*
denwa *telephone*
bangoo *number*
nan-ban *what number*

Calling up a friend at home

Brown	Moshi moshi, Satoo-san desu ka?
Woman	Hai, Satoo desu.
Brown	Taroo-san o onegai-shimasu.
Woman	Taroo wa ima ie ni imasen.
Brown	Soo desu ka. Dewa mata ato de denwa o kakemasu.

ima *now*
ie *house, home*
imasen *not be at, not exist*
ato de *later*
kakemasu *call up, hang*

The line is busy

Operator	Moshi moshi, Kinki Hoteru desu.
Brown	Go-hyaku san-goo-shitsu no Smith-san o onegai-shimasu.
Operator	Sumimasen ga, go-hyaku san-goo-shitsu wa hanashi-chuu desu.

go-hyasku san-goo-shitsu   *room number 503*
hanashi-chuu desu   *line is busy*

I can't hear you

Brown	Moshi moshi, Brown desu.
Woman	Tookyoo Ryokoosha desu ga, . . .
Brown	Yoku kikoemasen. Motto ookii koe de hanashite-kudasai.

ryokoosha   *travel agency*
yoku   *well*
kikoemasu   *can hear*
koe   *voice*
hanashimasu   *talk, speak*

Explanations

Negation of verbs

The negative form of **-masu** is **-masen**. For instance:

eat	tabemasu	tabemasen
go	ikimasu	ikimasen
buy	kaimasu	kaimasen
drink	nomimasu	nomimasen
is audible	kikoemasu	kikoemasen
see	mimasu	mimasen
is visible	miemasu	miemasen
exist	arimasu/imasu	arimasen/imasen

The negative form of **desu** is **dewa arimasen** or **ja arimasen**.

Arimasu vs. *imasu*

Arimasu express the existence of inanimate things, **imasu** of animate beings.

Heya ni beddo ga arimasu. *There is a bed in the room.*

Heya ni neko ga imasu. *There is a cat in the room.*

Either **imasu** or **arimasu** can be used to refer to the existence of family members.

Watashi wa kodomo ga arimasu/imasu. *I have a child/children.*

Time (2)

-Fun (**-pun** after the contracted forms of 1, 6 and 10, 3 **san**, and the question word **nan**) indicates the minute of the hour and also a duration of so many minutes.

ichi-ji juu-go-fun *1:15*   yo-ji ni-jup-pun *4:20*

Addressing a person

San is attached to either the first or the last name. **San** can correspond to Mr., Mrs., Miss, or Ms., but you cannot use it with your own name because it is an honorific expression.

Days of the week: See p. 65.

Particle *kara*

Kara indicates the starting point.

Go-ji kara shichi-ji made heya ni imasu. *I will be in my room from 5 to 7 o'clock.*

Amerika kara kimashita. *I came from America.*

Particle *ni*—place

Ni indicates the place where something or somebody exists.

Tomu wa heya ni imasen. *Tom is not in the room.*

Nihon ni yama ga
takusan arimasu.

*There are many mountains
in Japan.*

Particle *ni*—time

Ni indicates the time when an action or event takes
place.

Do-yoobi ni kaerimasu.   *I'll go home on Saturday.*

Exercises

1 Ima nan-ji desu ka? (What time is it now?)

a 7.30 P.M.   b 8:00 A.M.   c 4:15   d 6:45
e 10:20   f 11:50   g 9:35   h 2:40

2 Fill in the blanks. Can you find a place to stay
tonight for yourself and then for two of you?

a *You*   _____
   Receptionist Nan-nin desu ka?
   You   _____
   Receptionist Hai, gozaimasu.

b *You*   _____
   Receptionist Nan-nin desu ka?
   You   _____
   Receptionist Sumimasen ga, konban wa shinguru
                  no heya shika arimasen.

shika (followed by negation) *only*
shinguru *a room with a single bed*

3 Make a reservation at a restaurant:

a tonight, 7:30, two people
b tomorrow, lunch time, 12:00, three people (see
   Temporal terms, p. 47)

   at a hotel:

c Monday through Wednesday, next week, three
   nights, two adults

d from October 4, four nights, two adults and three children

4 Answer the following questions beginning your answer with **iie**:

a Hokkaidoo e ikimasu ka?

b (O)sake o nomimasu ka?

c Kamera o kaimasu ka?

d Yoyaku ga arimasu ka?

e Anata wa Nihon-jin desu ka?

anata *you*
-jin *people of . . .*

5 Yamada Hanako-san (Ms. Hanako Yamada) is your friend. She works at **kawase-ka** (the foreign exchange department) of **Taiheiyoo Ginkoo** (Taiheiyoo Bank). Call her up at her office.

a	*Operator*	Moshi moshi, Taiheiyoo Ginkoo desu.
	You	_____
	Operator	Hai, shooshoo omachi kudasai.
	Man	Moshi moshi, kawase-ka desu.
b	*You*	_____
	Man	Yamada wa kyoo wa yasumi desu.
c	*You*	_____

Then, call her up at her house.

d	*You*	_____
	Woman	Hai, soo desu.
e	*You*	_____
	Woman	Hai, chotto o-machi-kudasai.

Worth knowing

Hello and *moshi moshi*

"Hello" can be used for many occasions. **Moshi moshi**, however, is used only in a telephone conversation or when you're calling after someone you don't know in public, such as when a person leaves his or her umbrella behind on the train.

Americans say "hello" or "hi" even to an unfamiliar person as well as to friends; Japanese people do not usually greet people they do not know. (Greeting words are in Program 5.)

Public telephones

Smaller red telephones are designed only for local calls and take one 10-en coin at a time, though you can add 10-en coins one at a time during your conversation.

Bigger red telephones and blue telephones take several 10-en coins at a time for a local call or a long distance call. If your conversation does not cost as much as you have paid, the excess coins will be returned when you finish talking.

Yellow telephones are designed for long distance calls, though you can use them for local calls; they can take 100-en as well as 10-en coins. No coins are returned for 100-yen whether or not you have overpaid.

Green telephones take telephone cards as well as coins. You can purchase the cards at telephone companies or stores where green telephones are located for 500 en, 1,000 en, 3,000 en or 5,000 en.

Temporal terms

ima	*now*	ato de	*later*	mae ni	*before*
kyoo	*today*	ashita/asu	*tomorrow*	kinoo	*yesterday*

konshuu	*this week*	raishuu	*next week*	senshuu	*last week*
kongetsu	*this month*	raigetsu	*next month*	sengetsu	*last month*
kotoshi	*this year*	rainen	*next year*	kyonen	*last year*

asa	*morning*
(o)hiru	*noontime*
yuugata	*dusk*
yoru	*night; evening*
yonaka	*midnight*
kesa	*this morning*
konban	*this evening; tonight*

5 Staying at a Japanese inn

Key words

What is this?	**Kore wa nan desu ka?**
How do you say it in English?	**Ei-go de nan to iimasu ka?**
I want to swim.	**Oyogitai desu.**
Where is the best place to go?	**Doko e ittara, ii desu ka?**
No thank you.	**Moo kekkoo desu.**
Good morning.	**Ohayoo (gozaimasu).**
Good afternoon/Good day	**Konnichiwa**
Good evening	**Konbanwa**
Goodbye	**Sayoonara**
Have a good sleep/Good night (used when you leave someone at night)	**Oyasumi (nasai)**

Conversations

Arriving at an inn

Clerk   Irasshaimase.
Tourist   Konnichiwa. Brown desu.
Clerk   Doozo kochira e. (O)heya wa ni-kai no "Take no ma" desu.

-kai   *indicator for the floor*
Take no ma   *"Bamboo Room," the name of a room*
kochira   *this way, this direction, here*

Going to the room

Clerk   Koko desu. Doozo.
Tourist   Doomo arigatoo.
Clerk   Yuushoku wa nan-ji goro ga ii desu ka?

Tourist	Soo desu. Saki ni (o)furo ni hairitai desu kara, shichi-ji goro ni onegai-shimasu.
Clerk	Hai, wakarimashita. (O)furo wa (o)heya ni mo gozaimasu ga, daiyokujoo wa ik-kai desu.

yuushoku *supper*
goro *around (time)*
saki ni *at first*
(o)furo *bath*
hairimasu *enter*
kara *because*
mo *also, too*
gozaimasu *polite form of* arimasu
daiyokujoo *a big bath*

Having a meal in the room

Maid	Gomenkudasai. (O)shokuji no yooi ga dekimashita.
Tourist	Doozo.
Tourist	Itadakimasu.
Maid	Doozo.
Tourist	Kore wa nan desu ka?
Maid	Hirame no (o)sashimi desu.
Tourist	Oishii desu. Watashi wa sakana ga suki desu. "Hirame" wa Ei-go de nan to iimasu ka?
Maid	Sumimasen. Shirimasen.
Maid	Gohan no okawari wa ikaga desu ka?
Tourist	Moo kekkoo desu. Gochisoosama.

(o)shokuji *meal*
yooi ga dekimashita *be ready*
hirame *fluke*
(o)sashimi *a dish of raw fish*
oishii *tasty*
sakana *fish*
suki *be fond of*
shirimasen *not know*
gohan *cooked rice, meal*
okawari *second serving*

Having bedding prepared

Maid	(O)futon no yooi ga dekimashita.
	Oyasuminasaimase.
Tourist	Oyasumi.

futon *quilt*

In the morning in the hall

Clerk	Ohayoo gozaimasu, Buraun-san.
Tourist	Ohayoo.
Clerk	Kyoo wa dochira e?
Tourist	Umi de oyogitai desu. Doko e ittara, ii desu ka?
Clerk	Shirahama-kaigan ga ii desu yo.
Tourist	Shirahama-kaigan wa doo ittara, ii desu ka?
Clerk	Tonari no tabako-ya no mae de Misaki-iki no basu ni notte, Shirahama kaigan de orite kudasai.
Tourist	Wakarimashita. Jaa, ittekimasu.
Clerk	Itterasshaimase.

umi *sea*
oyogimasu *to swim*
kaigan *coast*
tonari *next door*
tabako-ya *tobacco shop*
mae *front*
norimasu *to get on*
orimasu *to get off*

Returning in the evening

Clerk	Okaerinasaimase.
Tourist	Tadaima.
Clerk	Umi wa doo deshita ka?
Tourist	Hito de ippai deshita. Dakara, amari oyogimasendeshita. Demo, kaigan no keshiki wa totemo kirei deshita. Shashin o takusan torimashita.

hito   *people*
ippai   *full*
dakara   *therefore*
amari . . .   *(negation); not much*
demo   *however*
keshiki   *scenery*
totemo   *very*
kirei   *pretty*
shashin   *photo*
takusan   *many, much*
torimasu   *to take*

Explanations

Expressing desire

Desire to do something can be expressed by combining **-tai (n) desu** with a certain form of a verb, which you can obtain by deleting **-masu** from the **-masu** form of a verb.

Umi de oyogitai desu.	*I want to swim in the sea.*
Furo ni hairitai desu.	*I want to take a bath.*

The particle **o** which marks the object may be replaced by **ga** in this construction, since **-tai** is no longer a verb but an adjective.

Sashimi ga/o tabetai desu.	*I want to eat sashimi.*
Uisukii ga/o nomitai desu.	*I want to drink whiskey.*

The desire to possess something is expressed by **hoshii desu**, and the object should be marked by **ga**.

Kamera ga hoshii desu.	*I want a camera.*
Jisho ga hoshii desu.	*I want a dictionary.*

Past tense form of verbs

-Masu becomes **-mashita** in the past tense.

Nara e ikimasu.	*I (will) go to Nara.*
Nara e ikimashita.	*I went to Nara.*

-Masen becomes **-masendeshita** in the past tense.

Kutsu o kaimasen.	*I do not buy shoes.*
Kutsu o kaimasendeshita.	*I did not buy shoes.*

Desu becomes **deshita** in the past tense.

Umi wa kirei desu.	*The sea is pretty.*
Umi wa kirei deshita.	*The sea was pretty.*

Dewa arimasen, or **ja arimasen**, negation of **desu**, becomes **dewa arimasendeshita** or **ja arimasendeshita**.

Hito de ippai dewa arimasen.	*It is not crowded with people.*
Hito de ippai dewa arimasendeshita.	*It was not crowded with people.*

Adjectives

There are two types of adjectives in Japanese: i-adjectives and na-adjectives.

All i adjectives end in -i in the present tense, plain form: **ookii, chiisai, akai, atsui, takai, oishii.**

They can modify nouns by themselves like English adjectives.

ookii kaban	*big bag*
atsui koohii	*hot coffee*

They conjugate. You can get the negative form by changing the final -i into **-kunai** in plain speech and **-kunai desu** in polite speech. **Ii** (good) is the one exception, and it becomes **yokunai (desu)**.

Kore wa oishikunai desu.	*This is not delicious.*
Kyoo wa atsukunai desu.	*It is not hot today.*

You form the past tense by changing -i into **-katta (desu)** and its negation by **-kunakatta (desu)**.

Kinoo wa samukatta desu.	*It was cold yesterday.*
Kore wa takakunakatta desu.	*This was not expensive.*

Na adjectives are few in number.

kirei	*pretty*	suki	*fond of*
joozu	*good at*	heta	*poor at*
kirai	*not fond of*	yuumei	*famous*

When these adjectives modify nouns, **na** appears between the adjectives and the nouns just as **no** appears between two nouns.

kirei na hito	*a pretty lady*
suki na sake	*favorite liquor*

Na adjectives do not conjugate and they behave like nouns. They are always followed by the **desu** verb as the predicate.

Keshiki wa kirei deshita.	*The scenery was beautiful.*
Nihon-go ga joozu dewa/ ja arimasen.	*I am not good at Japanese.*

Combining two sentences

Two sentences can be combined by changing the verb of the first sentence into a certain form.

Kono michi o massugu itte, shingoo o migi ni magarimasu.	*You go straight on this street and turn to the right at the traffic signal.*
Massugu ittara, ginkoo ga miemasu.	*If you go straight, you can see a bank.*

Two sentences can be combined into one by a conjunction.

Oishii desu kara, takusan tabemasu.	*Because it is delicious, I eat a lot.*
Oishii desu ga, amari tabemasen.	*It is delicious, but I do not eat much.*

Conjunctions such as **kara** and **ga** follow the first sentence, and cannot start a new sentence. On the other hand, conjunctive words like **dakara** and

demo cannot connect two sentences into one, but appear at the beginning of a sentence.

Oishii desu. Dakara takusan tabemasu.	*It is delicious. So, I'll eat a lot.*
Oishii desu. Demo, amari tabemasen.	*It is delicious. But, I won't eat much.*

Particle *ga*

Ga marks the object of adjectives and non-action verbs.

Watashi wa umi ga suki desu.	*I like the sea.*
Fuji-san ga miemasu.	*Mt. Fuji is visible.*
Jon wa Nihon-go ga wakarimasen.	*John does not understand Japanese.*

More greeting words

Ittekimasu	*Used by a member of a family (or such a group) when leaving home*
Itterasshai(mase)	*Used by a person at home when seeing off another member of the family*
Tadaima	*Used by a person when arriving home*
Okaeri(nasai; nasaimase)	*Used by a person at home to welcome home another member of the family*
Gomenkudasai	*Used by a person when entering someone else's house. (This can be used to attract the attention of a shopkeeper, if you enter a shop but see no one in attendance)*
Itadakimasu	*Used by a person when beginning to eat*
Gochisoosama	*Used by a person when finished eating*
Hajimemashite	*How do you do?*

Exercises

1 Greet your friend.

a *Friend* Ohayoo gozaimasu.
  You _____

b *Friend* Konnichiwa.
  You _____

c *Friend* Konbanwa.
  You _____

d *You* _____
  Friend Itterasshai.

e *You* _____
  Friend Okaerinasai.

f *Friend* Sayoonara.
  You _____

g *Friend* Oyasuminasai.
  You _____

2 Change the following sentences into . . . -**tai desu**, and ask, after each sentence, where is the best place to go.

a (O)hanami ni ikimasu.
  ((o)hanami *cherry blossom viewing*)

b Nihon no kimono o kaimasu.

c Oishii (o)sushi o tabemasu.

d Tanabata-matsuri o mimasu.
  (Tanabata-matsuri *Star Festival*)

e Ei-go no shinbun o yomimasu.
  (ei-go *English*; shinbun *newspaper*)

3 Connect the two sentences with kara.

a Atsui desu. Mado o akete-kudasai.
  (mado *window*)

b Kore wa chiisai desu. Motto ookii no o misete-kudasai.

c Daibutsu go mitai desu. Nara e ikimasu.
  (daibutsu *a great image of Buddha*)

d Fujisan ni noborimashita. Tsukaremashita.
  (noborimasu *climb*; tsukaremasu *get tired*)
e Hikooki ga kirai desu. Fune de kaerimasu.
  (hikooki *airplane*; fune *ship*; kaerimasu *go back*)

4 Change **ashita** into **kinoo** and complete the sentences.

a Ashita umi de oyogimasu.
b Ashita Kabuki o mimasu.
  (Kabuki *the Kabuki Theater*)
c Ashita otera no shashin o torimasu.
d Ashita sakana-tsuri o shimasen.
  (sakana-tsuri *fishing*; shimasu *do*)
e Ashita Chiba-eki de norikaemasen.

Worth knowing

Some Japanese customs

Taking off shoes

Japanese people do not wear shoes inside the house. There is an area called the **genkan**, where you take off your shoes, just inside the door of a house, apartment or Japanese-style inn (which is called a **ryokan** or **yadoya**). When you enter the inn, you may be provided with slippers to wear inside the building. You have to take off the slippers too when you enter a room covered with **tatami** (matting).

Japanese rooms

There is not much furniture in a Japanese room, so that one room can serve several different purposes. **Tatami** cover the floor. You sit on **zabuton** (cushions) on the floor and chat, write, read, or eat at the table.

After a meal, a maid cleans up the table and pushes it aside, and she prepares bedding (called a **futon**) on the floor so that you can sleep on it.

In the morning, the maid folds the bedding and puts it back in a closet before getting the table ready for breakfast.

Having meals in your own room

Dinner and breakfast are normally included in the cost of a room at a Japanese-style inn. Meals are served in your own room unless you are on a group tour and all members are going to dine together in a huge room.

Taking a bath

A Japanese bathtub is deeper than an American bathtub, and it is filled with very hot water. A bathroom, which is completely separate from the toilet, has a space next to the tub where you wash yourself with soap and rinse. Before soaking yourself in the tub, you have to rinse the soap off by pouring hot water over yourself from one of the basins that are always provided.

Can you GET BY?

Test

Try these exercises when you have finished the course. The answers are on page 70.

I Choose the correct answers.

1 One afternoon you meet a friend of yours. What do you say?

a Ohayoo
b Konnichiwa
c Konbanwa

2 You want to buy medicine. Where do you go?

a Kusuri-ya
b Pan-ya
c Hon-ya

3 At a restaurant you and Mr. White are going to have beer and Mrs. White a glass of red wine. How do you order?

a Biiru o ni-hai to aka-wain o ip-pon onegai-shimasu.
b Biiru o ni-hon to shiro-wain o ip-pai onegai-shimasu.
c Biiru o ni-hon to aka-wain o ip-pai onegai-shimasu.

4 You are going to buy a scarf. The salesperson said **san-zen rop-pyaku go-juu en desu**. How much is it?

a 3,650 yen
b 2,850 yen
c 3,450 yen

5 You are looking for a place to stay tonight. What do you say when you telephone a hotel?

a Moshi moshi, konban heya o kudasai.
b Moshi moshi, konban heya ga arimasu ka?
c Moshi moshi, konban heya ga doko desu ka?

6 You are looking for a post office. A passerby has told you **Kono michi o massugu itte, futatsu-me no kado o hidari ni magatta tokoro desu**. Which building is the post office?

A; B; C; D?

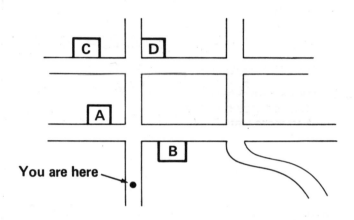

You are here

II Complete the conversation.

1 You want to see a Japanese garden, so you ask the receptionist where you should go
(niwa *garden*)

You _____

_____

Receptionist Kenrokuen ga ii desu yo.

2 You don't know where it is.

You _____

Receptionist Kanazawa ni arimasu.

3 How can you go there?

You   _____

Receptionist Koko kara densha de Kanazawa e itte, Kanazawa-eki no mae de Kenrokuen-iki no basu ni notte kudasai.

4 Now you understand

You   _____

5 At the station you have to buy tickets for you and your wife.

You   _____

Clerk   San-byaku ni-juu en desu.

6 At Kanazawa Station, you decide to take a taxi to Kenrokuen. But you can't find a taxi stand. Ask someone.

You   _____

Passerby   Sono kado o migi ni magatta tokoro desu.

7 You are in a taxi. Tell the driver where you want to go.

You   _____

Driver   Hai.

8 Wandering around in the garden, you have found an interesting object, but you can't figure out what it is. Ask someone.

You   _____

Passerby   Tooroo desu.

9 You don't know what **tooroo** is. She may know what it is called in English.

You   _____

Passerby   "Lantern" desu.

10 Now you know. Tell her so and thank her.

You   _____

11 Kanazawa is famous for pottery called **Kutani-yaki**. Go and buy some. In the shop, that one near the salesperson looks pretty. Ask her to show it to you.

You _____

Salesperson Hai, doozo.

12 It's pretty, isn't it?

You _____

13 But it might be too expensive. Ask her the price.

You _____

Salesperson Ni-sen go-hyaku en desu.

14 It's reasonable. Buy one for yourself and another for your friend.

You _____

Salesperson Doomo arigatoo gozaimasu.

15 Before going back to the inn, take a break at a coffee shop. Your wife wants coffee and pastry, but the menu does not say what kind of pastry they have. Ask the waitress.

You _____

Waitress Appuru-pai to chiizu-keeki to chokoreeto-keeki ga gozaimasu.

16 Your wife wants cheese cake. You just want coffee.

You _____

Waitress Hai, kashikomarimashita.

17 You are finally back at the inn.

Clerk Okaerinasaimase.

You _____

III Answer the following questions.

1 Ima nan-ji desu ka?
2 Anata wa Amerika-jin desu ka?
3 Itsu Nihon e kimashita ka?
   (itsu *when*; kimasu *to come*)
4 Doko kara kimashita ka?
5 Nihongo ga wakarimasu ka?
6 Nihon-ryoori ga suki desu ka?
   (ryori *cooking*)
7 Nihon de nani o kaimashita ka?
8 Nihon de doko e ikimashita ka?
9 Kabuki ga mitai desu ka?
10 Kono tesuto wa muzukashii desu ka?
   (tesuto *test*; muzukashii *difficult*)

Reference section

Numbers

0	zero; rei	100	hyaku
1	ichi	200	ni-hyaku
2	ni	300	san-byaku
3	san	400	yon-hyaku
4	yon; shi	500	go-hyaku
5	go	600	rop-pyaku
6	roku	700	nana-hyaku
7	shichi; nana	800	hap-pyaku
8	hachi	900	kyuu-hyaku
9	ku; kyuu	1000	sen
10	juu	2000	ni-sen
11	juu-ichi	3000	san-zen
12	juu-ni	4000	yon-sen
20	ni-juu	5000	go-sen
30	san-juu	6000	roku-sen
40	yon-juu	7000	nana-sen
50	go-juu	8000	has-sen
60	roku-juu	9000	kyuu-sen
70	nana-juu	10,000	ichi-man
80	hachi-juu	200,000	ni-juu-man
90	kyuu-juu	3,000,000	san-byaku-man
1983	sen kyuu-hyaku hachi-juu san		

Days of the week: -yoobi

Monday	**getsu-yoobi**	Friday	**kin-yoobi**
Tuesday	**ka-yoobi**	Saturday	**do-yoobi**
Wednesday	**sui-yoobi**	Sunday	**nichi-yoobi**
Thursday	**moku-yoobi**		

Days of the month: -nichi; -ka

1st **tsuitachi**	6th **muika**	11th **juu-ichi-nichi**
2nd **futsuka**	7th **nanoka**	12th **juu-ni-nichi**
3rd **mikka**	8th **yooka**	14th **juu-yokka**
4th **yokka**	9th **kokonoka**	20th **hatsuka**
5th **itsuka**	10th **tooka**	24th **ni-juu-yokka**

(*Note:* Omitted days are all followed by -nichi.)

Months of the year: -gatsu

Jan.	**ichi-gatsu**	July	**shichi-gatsu**
Feb.	**ni-gatsu**	Aug.	**hachi-gatsu**
Mar.	**san-gatsu**	Sept.	**ku-gatsu**
Apr.	**shi-gatsu**	Oct.	**juu-gatsu**
May	**go-gatsu**	Nov.	**juu-ichi-gatsu**
June	**roku-gatsu**	Dec.	**juu-ni-gatsu**

Useful addresses

American citizens must get visas for visits to Japan. Visas can be obtained from the embassy and consulates listed below.

Japanese Embassy
2520 Massachusetts Avenue, NW
Washington, D.C. 20008
Tel: (202) 234-2266

Consulates General of Japan
  909 West 9th Avenue, suite 301
  Anchorage AL 99501
  Tel: (907) 279-8428, 279-8429

  250 East First Street, suite 1507
  Los Angeles CA 90012
  Tel: (213) 624-8305

  1601 Post Street
  San Francisco CA 94115
  Tel: (415) 921-8000

  400 Colony Square Building, suite 1501
  1201 Peachtree Street, NE
  Atlanta GA 30361
  Tel: (404) 892-2700, 892-6670

1742 Nuuanu Avenue
Honolulu HA 96817
Tel: (808) 536-2226

625 North Michigan Avenue
Chicago IL 60611
Tel: (312) 280-0400

1830 International Trade Mart Building
No. 2 Canal Street
New Orleans LA 70130
Tel: (504) 529-2101, 529-2102

Federal Reserve Plaza, 14th floor
600 Atlantic Avenue
Boston MA 02210
Tel: (617) 973-9772/3/4

2519, Commerce Tower
911 Main Street
Kansas City MO 64105
Tel: (816) 471-0111/2/3

280 Park Avenue
New York NY 10017
Tel: (212) 986-1600

2400 First Interstate Tower
1300 SW 5th Avenue
Portland OR 97201
Tel: (503) 221-1811

1612 First City National Bank Building
1021 Main Street
Houston TX 77002
Tel: (713) 652-2977/8/9

Japan National Tourist Organization

The Japan National Tourist Organization provides free travel information. Its locations in the USA are as follows:

624 South Grand Avenue
Los Angeles CA 90017
Tel: (213) 623-1952

1737 Post Street
San Francisco CA 94115
Tel: (415) 931-0700

2270 Kalakaua Avenue
Honolulu, HA 96815
Tel: (808) 923-7631

333 North Michigan Avenue
Chicago IL 60601
Tel: (312) 332-3975

45 Rockefeller Plaza, 630 Fifth Avenue
New York NY 10111
Tel: (212) 757-5640

1519 Main Street, suite 200
Dallas, TX 75201
Tel: (214) 741-4931

Key to exercises

Chapter 1

1 _____ o onegai shimasu.
  a koohii   b aka-wain   c Sapporo biiru
  d aisukuriimu to koora   e keeki to koocha

2 a Koohii o mittsu onegai-shimasu.
  b Remon-tii o futatsu to koora o hitotsu onegai-shimasu.
  c Miruku-tii o hitotsu to tomato juusu o hitotsu to orenji juusu o
    futatsu onegai-shimasu.
  d Shiro wain o ip-pon onegai-shimasu.
  e Biiru o san-bon to uokka o ip-pai onegai-shimasu.

3 _____ wa nani ga arimasu ka?
  a aisukuriimu   b keeki   c supagetii   d sandoitchi   e dezaato

4 Sumimasen. Menyuu o onegai-shimasu.

Chapter 2

1 150   hyaku go-juu   260   ni-hyaku roku-juu
  370   san-byaku nana-juu 410   yon-hyaku juu
  1600 sen rop-pyaku   3520 san-zen go-hyaku ni-juu
  4090 yon-sen kyuu-juu   5700 go-sen nana-hyaku
  8880 has-sen hap-pyaku hachi-juu

2 a Nihon-shu/(o)sake o ni-hon kudasai.
  b Hamu o san-byaku-guramu kudasai.
  c Gureepufuruutsu o yottsu kudasai.
  d Go-hyaku-en-kitte o ni-mai kudasai.
  e Kookuushokan o juu-mai kudasai.

3 _____ o misete-kudasai.
  a sore   b are   c akai no   d kuroi no   e aoi no
  f motto chiisai no   g motto karui no   h motto yasui no

4 a Are o misete-kudasai.   b Ni-juu has-senchi desu.
  c Chotto chiisai desu.   d Motto ookii no o misete-kudasai.
  e Ikura desu ka?

5 a Senbin de onegai-shimasu.
  b Kookuubin de ikura desu ka?
  c Doru ni kaete-kudasai.

Chapter 3

1 a Oosaka made otona ni-mai, kodomo ni-mai.
  b Sendai made otona ichi-mai, kodomo san-mai.
  c Kamakura made otona yon-mai, kodomo roku-mai.
  d Nara made otona go-mai, kodomo ichi-mai.
  e San-ji-hatsu no Kodama no kippu, Kyooto made otona ichi-mai, kodomo ichi-mai.

2 a Takushii-noriba wa doko desu ka? (Over there.)
  b Toire wa doko desu ka? (It's inside the station.)
  c Yuubinkyoko wa doko desu ka? (It's where you go straight on this street to the third corner.)
  d Ginkoo wa doko desu ka? (It's where you go straight on this street, turn to the left at the second signal, and walk about 100 meters.)
  e Sagano-iki no basu no noriba wa doko desu ka? (It's where you turn left at that corner.)

3 a Yasaka-jinja wa doo ittara, ii desu ka? (Go straight on this street, turn to the right at the second signal and then turn to the left at the first corner.)
  b Arashiyama wa doo ittara, ii desu ka? (Go to Katsura by this train and change to the train for Arashiyama at Katsura.)

Chapter 4

1 a gogo shichi-ji han   b gozen hachi-ji   c yo-ji juu-go-fun
  d roku-ji yon-juu-go-fun   e juu-ji ni-jup-pun
  f juu-ichi-ji go-jup-pun   g ku-ji san-juu-go-fun
  h ni-ji yon-jup-pun

2 a Konban; heya ga arimasu ka?   Hitori desu.
  b Konban heya ga arimasu ka?   Futari desu.

3 a Konban shichi-ji-han ni futari yoyaku o onegai-shimasu.
  b Ashita no (o)hiru juu-ni-ji ni san-nin yoyaku o onegai-shimasu.
  c Raishuu no getsu-yoobi kara sui-yoobi made, san-paku, otona futari yoyaku o onegai-shimasu.
  d Juu-gatsu yokka kara yon-paku, otona futari to kodomo san-nin yoyaku o onegai-shimasu.

4 a Iie, ikimasen. b Iie, nomimasen. c Iie, kaimasen.
  d Iie, arimasen. e Iie, watashi wa Nihon-jin dewa arimasen.

5 a Kawase-ka no Yamada-san o onegai-shimasu.
  b Yamada-san o onegai-shimasu.
  c Soo desu ka. Wakarimashita.
  d Moshi moshi, Yamada-san desu ka?
  e Hanako-san o onegai-shimasu.

Chapter 5

1 a Ohayoo (gozaimasu) b konnichiwa c Konbanwa
d Ittekimasu e Tadaima f Sayoonara g Oyasumi (nasai)

2 a (O)hanami ni ikitai desu. Doko e ittara, ii desu ka?
b Nihon no kimono ga/o kaitai desu. Doko e ittara, ii desu ka?
c Oishii (o)sushi ga/o tabetai desu. Doko e ittara, ii desu ka?
d Tanabata-matsuri ga/o mitai desu. Doko e ittara, ii desu ka?
e Ei-go no shinbun ga/o yomitai desu. Doko e ittara, ii desu ka?

3 a Atsui desu kara, mado o akete-kudasai.
b Kore wa chiisai desu kara, motto ookii no o misete-kudasai.
c Daibutsu ga mitai desu kara, Nara e ikimasu.
d Fujisan ni noborimashita kara, tsukaremashita.
e Hikooki ga kirai desu kara, fune de kaerimasu.

4 a Kinoo umi de oyogimashita.
b Kinoo Kabuki o mimashita.
c Kinoo otera no shashin o torimashita.
d Kinoo sakana-tsuri o shimasendeshita.
e Kinoo Chiba-eki de norikaemasendeshita.

Answers to Can You GET BY?

I 1 b 2 a 3 c 4 a 5 b 6 c

II 1 Nihon no niwa ga mitai desu. Doko e ittara, ii desu ka?
2 Kenrokuen wa doko ni arimasu ka?
3 Doo ittara, ii desu ka?
4 Wakarimashita. Doomo arigatoo.
5 Kanazawa made otona ni-mai.
6 Sumimasen. Takushii-noriba wa doko desu ka?
7 Kenrokuen e itte-kudasai.
8 Sumimasen. Are wa nan desu ka?
9 "Tooroo" wa Ei-go de nan to iimasu ka?
10 Wakarimashita. Doomo arigatoo.
11 Sore o misete-kudasai.
12 Kirei desu ne.
13 Ikura desu ka?
14 Kore o futatsu kudasai.
15 Keeki wa nani ga arimasu ka?
16 Chiizu-keeki o hitotsu to koohii o futatsu onegai-shimasu.
17 Tadaima.

III (sample answers)

1 Ni-ji han desu.
2 Hai, soo desu. / Iie, chigaimasu.
3 Hachi-gatsu juu-go-nichi ni kimashita. / Do-yoobi ni kimashita.
4 Amerika kara kimashita.

5 Hai, sukoshi (*a little*) wakarimasu. / Iie, wakarimasen.
6 Hai, suki desu. / Iie, kirai desu.
7 Kamera to ningyoo (*doll*) o kaimashita.
8 Kyooto to Nara to Kagoshima e ikimashita.
9 Hai, mitai desu. / Iie, mitakunai desu.
10 Hai, muzukashii desu. / Iie, muzukashikunai desu.

Japanese-English word list

All translations given are as used in this book. Verbs are listed in
-**masu** forms followed by -**te** forms in parens. Nouns are preceded
by **o** or **go** in parens if the form is almost equally acceptable in any
speech either with or without the prefix. Honorific forms are
marked (H).

A

aisu *ice*
aisu-koohii *iced coffee*
aisu-tii *iced tea*
aisukuriimu *ice cream*
aka *red(ness)*
akai *red*
akemasu (akete) *open*
amai *sweet*
amari . . . (negation) *not much*
Amerika *U.S.A.*
Amerikan koohii *American coffee*
anata *you*
annai-sho *information center/desk*
ano *that (adjectival use)*
aoi *blue; green*
appuru-pai *apple pie*
are *that over there*
arigatoo (gozaimasu/-mashita) *thank you*
arimasu (atte) *exist (inanimate objects)*
asa *morning*
asa-gohan *breakfast*
ashita *tomorrow*
asoko *over there*
asu *tomorrow*
ato de *later*
atsui *hot (temperature)*

B

-bai *(counter suffix for glasses of liquid)*
ban-gohan *supper*
bangoo *number*
-ban-me *(suffix to make an ordinal number)*
basu *bus*
beddo *bed*
biiru *beer*
bijutsu-kan *art museum*
biyooin *beauty salon*
-bon *(counter suffix for long, slender objects)*
-byaku *unit of hundred*
byooin *hospital*

C

(o)cha *tea*
chigaimasu (chigatte) *is wrong; is different*
chiisai *small*
chiizu-keeki *cheesecake*
chikatetsu *subway*
chizu *map*
chokoreeto-keeki *chocolate cake*
choodo *just; exactly*
chooshoku *breakfast*
chotto *a little*
chuushoku *lunch*

D

daburu *room with a double bed*
daibutsu *great image of Buddha*
daiyokujoo *big bath*
dakara *therefore; so*
de *(indicates the place where an action takes places) at; in*
de *(indicates the means) by; with*
dekimasu (dekite) *become ready; can do*
demo *however; but*
densha *train*
denwa *telephone*
denwa-bangoo *telephone number*
depaato *department store*
deshita *was/were*
desu *is/am/are*
dewa *well; then*
dewa arimasen *is/am/are not*
dezaato *dessert*
do *degree*
doa *door*
dochira *which way; where*
doko *where*
doo *how*
doobutsuen *zoo*
doo itashimashite *Don't mention it; you're welcome*
doomo *very much*
doozo *please*
dore *which*
doroboo *burglar*
doru *dollar*
do-yoobi *Saturday*

E

e *(indicates direction) to; toward*
eiga *movie*
eiga-kan *movie theatre*
Ei-go *English*
eki *station*
en *yen*

F

-fun *minute*
fune *ship*

(o)furo *bath*
futari *two people*
futatsu *two*
futon *quilt*

G

ga *but*
ga *(indicates the subject of a sentence)*
-gakari *a person or section in charge of*
gasorin sutando *gas station*
-gatsu *month of the year*
gekijoo *theater*
getsu-yoobi *Monday*
ginkoo *bank*
go *five*
gochisoosama *greeting word when one finishes eating*
gogo *p.m.; afternoon*
gohan *cooked rice; meal*
gomenkudasai *greeting word when one enters someone's house*
-goo-shitsu *room number*
goro *around (time)*
gozaimasu *(polite form of arimasu/desu)*
gozen *a.m.*
gurai *about (quantity)*
guramu *gram*
gureepufuruutsu *grapefruit*
gyuunyuu *milk*

H

hachi *eight*
hai *yes*
-hai *(counter suffix for glasses of liquid)*
hairimasu (haitte) *enter*
hajimemashite *How do you do?*
-haku *(counter suffix for nights to stay)*
hakubutsukan *museum*
hamu *ham*
(o)hanami *cherry-blossom viewing*
-han *half-past*

hanashi-chuu *telephone line is busy*

hanashimasu (hanashite) *talk; speak*

(o)hashi *chopstick*

-hatsu *(indicates the departure time)*

heta *poor at*

heya *room*

hidari *left*

hikooki *airplane*

hikui *low*

hirame *fluke*

(o)hiru *noon*

(o)hiru-gohan *lunch*

hito *person*

hitori *one person*

hitotsu *one*

-hon *(counter suffix for long, slender things)*

hon *book*

hon-ya *bookstore*

hoshii *want*

hoteru *hotel*

hotto-keeki *pancake*

hyakkaten *department store*

hyaku *hundred*

I

ichi *one*

ichi-gatsu *January*

ichigo-jamu *strawberry jam*

ie *house; home*

ii *good*

iie *no*

iimasu (itte) *say; call*

ikaga *how; how about*

-iki *(indicates the destination)*

ikimasu (itte) *go*

ima *now*

imasu (ite) *exist (animate beings)*

ippai *full*

irasshaimase *welcome*

isha *doctor*

itadakimasu *greeting word when one begins to eat*

itsu *when*

itsutsu *five*

ittekimasu *greeting word when one leaves home*

itterasshai *greeting word when one sees someone off from home*

J

jaa *well,*

ja arimasen *is/am/are not*

jamu *jam*

-ji *o'clock*

-jin *people of (nationality)*

jinja *shrine*

jinji-ka *personnel section*

jisho *dictionary*

joozu *good at*

juu *ten*

juu-gatsu *October*

juu-ichi-gatsu *November*

juu-ni-gatsu *December*

K

ka *(marker for a question sentence)*

kaban *bag*

kado *corner*

kaemasu (kaete) *exchange*

kaerimasu (kaette) *return; go home*

-kai *floor*

kaigan *coast*

kaimasu (katte) *buy*

kaji *fire*

kakemasu *hang*

kakemasu, denwa o *telephone*

kakimasu (kaite) *write*

kamera *camera*

(o)kanjoo *bill*

kara *(indicates the starting point of time, place)*

kara *because*

karai *salty, spicy*

karui *light; not heavy*

kashikomarimashita *yes, certainly*

(o)kashi-ya *snack shop*

kawase-ka *foreign exchange department*

ka-yoobi *Tuesday*

keeki *cake*
keisatsu *police*
kesa *this morning*
keshiki *scenery*
kiiroi *yellow*
kikimasu (kiite) *listen; ask*
kikoemasu (kikoete) *can hear; audible*
kimasu (kite) *come*
kimono *kimono*
kinoo *yesterday*
kin-yoobi *Friday*
kippu *ticket*
kirai *dislike*
kirei *pretty; beautiful*
kiroguramu *kilogram*
kiromeetoru *kilometer*
kissaten *coffee shop*
kitte *postal stamp*
kochira *this way; here*
kodomo *child*
koe *voice*
koko *here*
kokoa *cocoa; hot chocolate*
kokonotsu *nine*
konban *tonight*
konbanwa *good evening*
kongetsu *this month*
konnichiwa *good afternoon*
kono *this (adjectival use)*
konshuu *this week*
koocha *black tea*
kooen *park*
koohii *coffee*
kookuubin *airmail*
kookuushokan *aerogram*
koora *coke*
kore *this*
kotoshi *this year*
ku *nine*
kudasai *give me*
ku-gatsu *September*
kuriimu-sooda *ice-cream soda*
kuro-biiru *dark beer*
kuroi *black*
kusuri *medicine*
kusuri-ya *drugstore*
kutsu *shoe*
kyonen *last year*

kyoo *today*
kyookai *church*
kyuu *nine*
kyuukyuusha *ambulance*

M

maamareedo *marmalade*
machimasu (matte) *wait*
made *(indicates limit of time, place)*
mado *window*
mae *front*
mae ni *before*
magarimasu (magatte) *turn*
-mai *(counter suffix for thin, flat objects)*
man *ten thousand*
man'in *booked up; full with people*
(o)manjuu *Japanese sweet pastry*
mantan *full tank*
maruku *mark (German currency)*
massugu *straight*
mata *again*
-me *(marker for ordinal numbers)*
menyuu *menu*
michi *way; street; road*
miemasu (miete) *can see; visible*
migi *right*
mijikai *short*
mikka *third day of the month*
mikkusu *assorted*
mimasu (mite) *see; watch*
minna *all; everybody*
misemasu (misete) *show*
miruku *milk*
miruku-tii *tea with cream*
mittsu *three*
mizu *water*
mo *also; too*
moku-yoobi *Thursday*
moo kekkoo desu *no thank you*
moshi moshi *hello (on the phone)*
motto *more*
muttsu *six*
muzukashii *difficult*

N

nagai *long*
naka *inside*
nama-biiru *draft beer*
namae, o namae (H) *name*
nan, nani *what*
nana *seven*
nanatsu *seven*
ne *(tag question)*
neko *cat*
ni *two*
ni *(indicates the place of existence)*
ni *(indicates the time when action takes place)* at; on
ni *(indicates destination)*
nichi-yoobi *Sunday*
nigai *bitter*
Nihon *Japan*
Nihon-cha *Japanese green tea*
Nihon-go *Japanese language*
Nihon-shu *Japanese rice wine*
niku-ya *meat market*
-nin *(counter suffix for people)*
ningyoo *doll*
niwa *garden; yard*
no *(follows noun which modifies another noun)*
no *(substitutes for nouns when they are preceded by adjectives, pronouns, proper names)*
noborimasu (nobotte) *climb;*
nomimasu (nonde) *drink*
noriba *place where one boards a vehicle*
norikaemasu (norikaete) *transfer*

O

o *(indicates the object of a sentence)*
o *(indicates the place where motion takes place)* at; in; on
(o)cha *tea*
ohayoo (gozaimasu) *good morning*
oishii *tasty*
okaeri(nasai) *greeting word when one welcomes another member of the family home*

okawari *second serving*
o-machi-kudasai (H) *please wait*
omoi *heavy*
onegai-shimasu (-shite) *please; ask a favor*
ookii *big; large*
orenji-juusu *orange juice*
orimasu (orite) *get off; go down*
oshiemasu (oshiete) *teach, inform*
oshiemasu, michi o *show the way*
o tearai *toilet*
otona *adult*
oyogimasu (oyoide) *swim*

P

-paku *(counter suffix for nights to stay)*
pan *bread*
pan-ya *bakery*
-pon *(counter suffix for long, slender objects)*
pondo *pound (British currency)*
-pun *minute*
purin *custard*
-pyaku *unit of hundred*

R

raigetsu *next month*
rainen *next year*
raishuu *next week*
rei *zero*
remoneedo *lemonade*
remon-tii *tea with lemon*
resutoran *restaurant*
rittoru *liter*
roku *six*
roku-gatsu *June*
ryokan *Japanese-style inn*
ryokoo-sha *travel agent*
ryoojikan *consulate*
ryoori *cooking*

S

saizu *size*
sakana *fish*
sakana-tsuri *fishing*
sakana-ya *fish market*

(o)sake *Japanese rice wine; liquor*
saki ni *first*
samui *cold (weather)*
san *three*
-san (H) *Mr.; Mrs.; Miss; Ms.*
sandoitchi *sandwich*
san-gatsu *March*
(o)sashimi *dish of raw fish*
satoo *sugar*
sayoonara *goodby*
sen *thousand*
senbin *surface mail*
senchi(meetoru) *centimeter*
sengetsu *last month*
senshuu *last week*
shashin *photo*
shi *four*
shi-gatsu *April*
shichi *seven*
shichi-gatsu *July*
shika (negation) *only*
shimasu (shite) *do*
shinbun *newspaper*
shingoo *traffic light*
shinguru *room with a single bed*
shirimasu (shitte); shirimasen;
shitte imasu *get to know; not
know; know*
shiro *white(ness)*
shiroi *white*
shokubutsuen *botanical garden*
(o)shokuji *meal*
shooji-gaisha *trading company*
shooshoo *a little*
soko *there; that place*
sono *that (adjectival use)*
soo *so*
sooda *soda*
sore *that; that one*
sorekara *then*
sui-yoobi *Wednesday*
suki *like*
sumimasen *excuse me; I'm
sorry; thank you*
supagetti *spaghetti*
suri *pickpocket*
suupaa *supermarket*
(o)sushi *sushi*

T

tabako *cigarette; cigar*
tabako-ya *tobacco shop*
tabemasu (tabete) *eat*
taishikan *embassy*
takai *high; expensive*
takusan *many; much*
takushii *taxi*
tamago *egg*
Tasukete! *Help!*
(o)tera *temple*
tesuto *test*
to *(connects two nouns); and*
toire *toilet*
tokoro *place*
tomato-juusu *tomato juice*
tonari *next door*
too *ten*
tooroo *lantern*
toosuto *toast*
torimasu (totte) *take*
totemo *very*
tsuin *room with twin beds*
tsukaremasu (tsukarete) *get
tired*
tsumetai *cold (drinks, food)*

U

uinnaa koohii *Viennese coffee*
uisukii *whiskey*
umi *sea*
uokka *vodka*
uriba *selling place*

W

wain *wine*
wakarimasu (wakatte)
understand
watashi *I*

Y

yadoya *Japanese-style inn*
yama *mountain*
yao-ya *green grocer*
yasai *vegetable*
yasui *inexpensive*
yasumi *vacation; absence*
yattsu *eight*

yobimasu (yonde) *call; invite*
yoku *well*
yomimasu (yonde) *read*
yon *four*
yonaka *midnight*
-yoobi *day of the week*
yooi *preparation*
yoru *night*
yottsu *four*

yoyaku *reservation*
yuubinkyoku *post office*
yuugata *dusk*
yuumei *famous*
yuushoku *supper*

Z
-zen *unit of a thousand*
zero *zero*

English-Japanese word list

A
able *dekimasu*
absence *yasumi*
adult *otona*
aerogram *kookuushokan*
again *mata*
airmail *kookuubin*
airplane *hikooki*
all *minna*
also *mo*
a.m. *gozen*
am *desu*
ambulance *kyuukuusha*
America *Amerika*
American coffee *Amerikan koohii*
and *to*
apple pie *appuru-pai*
April *shi-gatsu*
approximately (time) *goro*; (quantity) *gurai*
are *desu*
art museum *bijutsukan*
as far as *made*
ask *kikimasu*
assorted *mikkusu*
at (place) *de* (time) *ni*
audible *kikoemasu*

B
bag *kaban*
bakery *pan-ya*
bank *ginkoo*
bath *(o) furo*
 big bath *daiyokujoo*

beautiful *kirei*
beauty salon *biyooin*
because *kara*
beer *biiru*
 dark beer *kuro-biiru*
 draft beer *nama-biiru*
bed *beddo*
before *mae ni*
big *ookii*
bill *(o)kanjoo*
bitter *nigai*
black *kuroi*
blue *aoi*
book *hon*
bookstore *hon-ya*
botanical garden *shokubutsuen*
bread *pan*
brakfast *asa-gohan; chooshoku*
burglar *doroboo*
buy *kaimasu*
but *demo; ga*

C
cake *keeki*
call *yobimasu*
call up (telephone) *denwa o kakemasu*
camera *kamera*
cat *neko*
centimeter *senchi(meetoru)*
cheesecake *chiizu-keeki*
cherry-blossom viewing *(o)hanami*
child *kodomo*
chocolate cake *chokoreeto-keeki*

chopsticks *(o)hashi*
church *kyookai*
cigarette *tabako*
cigarette shop *tabako-ya*
climb *noborimasu*
coast *kaigan*
cocoa *kokoa*
coffee *koohii*
  Viennesse coffee
  uinnaa koohii
coffee shop *kissaten*
cold (weather) *samui*
  (drink, food) *tsumetai*
coke *koora*
come *kimasu*
consulate *ryoojikan*
cooking *ryoori*
corner *kado*
custard *purin*

D

December *juu-ni-gatsu*
department store *depaato;
hyakkaten*
dessert *dezaato*
dictionary *jisho*
different *chigaimasu*
difficult *muzukashii*
dislike *kirai*
do *shimasu*
doctor *isha*
doll *ningyoo*
dollar *doru*
door *doa*
drink *nomimasu*
drugstore *kusuri-ya*
dusk *yuugata*

E

eat *tabemasu*
egg *tamago*
eight *hachi; yattsu*
embassy *taishikan*
English *Ei-go*
enter *hairimasu*
everyone *minna*
exactly *choodo*
exchange *kaemasu*
excuse me *sumimasen*

exist (inanimate)
(animate) *arimasu; imasu*
expensive *takai*

F

famous *yuumei*
February *ni-gatsu*
first *saki ni*
fish *sakana*
fish market *sakana-ya*
fishing *sakana-tsuri*
five *go; itsutsu*
floor *-kai/-gai*
fluke *hirame*
foreign exchange
department *kawase-ka*
four *yon/shi; yottsu*
front *mae*
full *ippai*
full tank *mantan*
full with people *man'in*

G

garden *niwa; teien*
gas station *gasorin sutando*
get off *orimasu*
get on *norimasu*
get tired *tsukaremasu*
give me, please *kudasai*
go *ikimasu*
go down *orimasu*
go home *kaerimasu*
go up *noborimasu*
good *ii*
good at *joozu*
goodby *sayoonara*
good morning *ohayoo
(gozaimasu)*
gram *guramu*
grapefruit *gureepufuruutsu*
green *aoi*
green grocer *yao-ya*

H

half *han*
ham *hamu*
hang *kakemasu*
hear *kikimasu*
heavy *omoi*

hello (on the phone) *moshi moshi*
Help! *Tasukete!*
here *koko; kochira*
high *takai*
home *ie*
hospital *byooin*
hot (temperature) *atsui*
 (spicy) *karai*
hot chocolate *kokoa*
hotel *hoteru*
house *ie*
how *doo; ikaga*
however *demo*
hundred *hyaku/-byaku/-pyaku*

I

I *watashi*
ice *koori*
ice cream *aisukuriimu*
iced coffee *aisu-koohii*
iced tea *aisu-tii*
in *ni; de*
inform *oshiemasu*
information center/desk *annai-sho*
inside *naka*
is *desu*

J

jam *jamu*
January *ichi-gatsu*
Japan *Nihon*
Japanese (language) *Nihon-go*
Japanese green tea *(o)cha*
Japanese rice wine *(o)sake*
Japanese-style inn *yadoya; ryokan*
Japanese sweet pastry *(o)manjuu*
July *shichi-gatsu*
June *roku-gatsu*

K

kilogram *kiroguramu*
kilometer *kiromeetoru*
know *shitte-imasu*
 get to know *shirimasu*
 do not know *shirimasen*

L

lantern *tooroo*
last month *sengetsu*
last week *senshuu*
last year *kyonen*
later *ato de*
left *hidari*
lemonade *remoneedo*
like *suki*
light (not heavy) *karui*
liquor *(o)sake*
listen *kikimasu*
liter *rittoru*
(little) a little *chotto; shooshoo*
long *nagai*
look *mimasu*
low *hikui*
lunch *(o)hiru-gohan; chuushoku*

M

many *takusan*
map *chizu*
March *san-gatsu*
mark (German currency) *maruku*
marmalade *maamareedo*
May *go-gatsu*
meal *gohan; (o)shokuji*
meat *niku*
meat market *niku-ya*
medicine *kusuri*
(mention) Don't mention it *Doo itashimashite*
menu *menyuu*
midnight *yonaka*
milk *miruku; gyuunyuu*
minute *-fun/-pun*
Miss *-san (H)*
Monday *getsu-yoobi*
more *motto*
morning *asa*
 this morning *kesa*
mountain *yama*
movie *eiga*
movie theater *eiga-kan*
Mr. *-san (H)*
Mrs. *-san (H)*
much *takusan*
 not much *amari . . .* (negation)

museum *hakubutsu-kan*

N

name *namae; o namae* (H)
newspaper *shinbun*
next door *tonari*
next month *raigetsu*
next week *raishuu*
next year *rainen*
night *yoru*
nine *ku/kyuu; kokonotsu*
no *iie*
no thank you *moo kekkoo desu*
noon *(o)hiru*
not
  is/are/am not *dewa/ja arimasen*
  do/does not Verb *-masen*
  was/were not *dewa/ja arimasendeshita*
  did not Verb *-masendeshita*
November *juu-ichi-gatsu*
now *ima*
number *bangoo*

O

October *juu-gatsu*
on (place) *ni; de; o*
  (time) *ni*
one *ichi; hitotsu*
only *shika . . . (negation)*
open *akemasu*
orange juice *orenji-juusu*

P

pancake *hottokeeki*
park *kooen*
people of (nationality) *-jin*
person *hito*
pharmacy *kusuri-ya*
photo *shashin*
pickpocket *suri*
please *doozo; onegai-shimasu*
place *tokoro*
police *keisatsu*
poor at *heta*
post office *yuubinkyoku*

pound *pondo*
preparation *yooi*
pretty *kirei*

Q

quilt *futon*

R

raw fish *(o)sashimi*
read *yomimasu*
ready (done) *dekimasu*
red *akai*
red(ness) *aka*
reservation *yoyaku*
restaurant *resutoran*
return *kaerimasu*
rice (cooked) *gohan*
rice wine *(o)sake*
right *migi*
road *michi*
room *heya*

S

salt *shio*
salty *karai*
sandwich *sandoitchi*
Saturday *do-yoobi*
say *iimasu*
scenery *keshiki*
sea *umi*
see *mimasu*
second serving *okawari*
selling place *uriba*
September *ku-gatsu*
seven *shichi/nana; nanatsu*
ship *fune*
shoe *kutsu*
short *mijikai*
show *misemasu*
shrine *jinja*
six *roku; muttsu*
size *saizu*
small *chiisai*
snack shop *(o)kashi-ya*
so *soo*
soda *sooda*
sorry *sumimasen*
spaghetti *supagetti*

speak *hanashimasu*
spicy *karai*
stamp *kitte*
station *eki*
store *mise*
straight *massugu*
strawberry jam *ichigo-jamu*
street *michi*
subway *chikatetsu*
sugar *satoo*
Sunday *nichi-yoobi*
supermarket *suupaa*
supper *ban-gohan; yuushoku*
surface mail *senbin*
sweet *amai*
swim *oyogimasu*

T
take *torimasu*
talk *hanashimasu*
tasty *oishii*
taxi *takushii*
tea *(o)cha*
  black tea *koocha*
  green tea *(o)cha; Nihon-cha*
  tea with cream *miruku-tii*
  tea with lemon *remon-tii*
teach *oshiemasu*
telephone *denwa*
telephone number *denwa-bangoo*
temple *(o)tera*
ten *juu; too*
ten thousand *man*
test *tesuto*
thank you *arigatoo (gozaimasu/-mashita)*
that *sore*
  (adjectival use) *sono*
that over there *are*
  (adjectival use) *ano*
theater *gekijoo*
then *sore kara*
there; over there *soko; asoko*
therefore *dakara*
this *kore*
  (adjectival use) *kono*
this month *kongetsu*

this morning *kesa*
this week *konshuu*
this year *kotoshi*
thousand *(-)sen/-zen*
three *san; mittsu*
Thursday *moku-yoobi*
ticket *kippu*
toast *toosuto*
today *kyoo*
toilet *toire; otearai*
tomato juice *tomato-juusu*
tomorrow *asu; ashita*
tonight *konban*
too *mo*
toward *e; ni*
trading company *shooji-gaisha*
traffic light *shingoo*
train *densha*
transfer *norikaemasu*
travel agent *ryokoo-sha*
Tuesday *ka-yoobi*
turn *magarimasu*
two *ni; futatsu*

U
understand *wakarimasu*
until *made*
USA *Amerika*

V
vacation *yasumi*
vegetable *yasai*
very *totemo*
visible *miemasu*
vodka *uokka*
voice *koe*

W
wait *machimasu*
want *hoshii*
want to (verb) *-tai desu*
water *mizu*
way *michi*
Wednesday *sui-yoobi*
welcome *irasshaimase*
  You're welcome *doo itashimashite*
well *yoku*

Well, . . . *Jaa; Dewa* . . .
what *nani; nan*
when *itsu*
where *doko; dochira*
which *dore; dochira*
white *shiroi*
white(ness) *shiro*
whiskey *uisukii*
window *mado*
wine *wain*
write *kakimasu*
wrong *chigaimasu*

Y

yellow *kiiroi*
yen *en*
yes *hai*
yesterday *kinoo*
you *anata*

Z

zero *zero; rei*
zoo *doobutsuen*

Useful signs to recognize

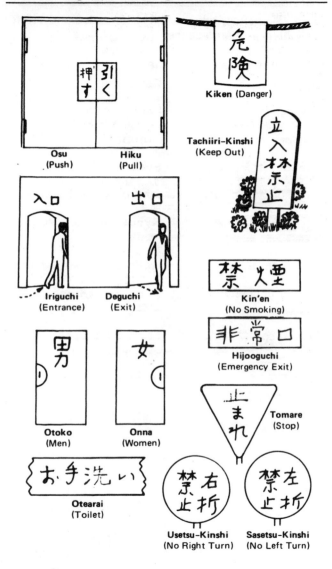

Osu
(Push)

Hiku
(Pull)

Kiken (Danger)

Tachiiri-Kinshi
(Keep Out)

Iriguchi
(Entrance)

Deguchi
(Exit)

Kin'en
(No Smoking)

Hijooguchi
(Emergency Exit)

Otoko
(Men)

Onna
(Women)

Tomare
(Stop)

Otearai
(Toilet)

Usetsu-Kinshi
(No Right Turn)

Sasetsu-Kinshi
(No Left Turn)

Panic situations

In an emergency, telephone 110 for police and 119 for firefighters and ambulance.

Words and phrases you may need in a hurry

Help!	**Tasukete!** 助けて//
Fire!	**Kaji!** 火 事//
Burglar!	**Doroboo!** 泥 棒//
Pickpocket!	**Suri!** す り//
Call a doctor, please.	**Isha o yonde kudasai.** 医者を呼んでください。
Call an ambulance, please.	**Kyuukyuusha o yonde kudasai.** 救急車を呼んでください。
Where am I?	**Koko wa doko desu ka?** ここは どこですか。
Do you understand English?	**Ei-go wakarimasu ka?** 英語が分かりますか。
Do you speak English?	**Ei-go o hanashimasu ka?** 英語を話しますか。

Japan travel-phone

In Japan, Tourist Information Centers (T.I.C.) provide English-language assistance and travel information service over the telephone from 9:00 a.m. through 5:00 p.m. seven days a week. The toll-free number is 106 except in Tokyo and Kyoto. If you use a public telephone, use either a yellow or blue one (not a red one), insert a ten en coin, dial 106 and tell the operator, "Collect call, T.I.C." The coin will be returned after your call. This service is available through private telephones, too.

If you are in Tokyo, dial 502-1461 for Tokyo T.I.C. In Kyoto, telephone 371-5649 for Kyoto T.I.C. These telephone numbers are not toll-free and the charge is ten en per three minutes.

ITINERARY

DATE	PLACE

EXPENSES

DATE	AMT.	U.S.$	FOR:

EXPENSES

DATE	AMT.	U.S.$	FOR:

PURCHASES

ITEM _____

WHERE BOUGHT _____

GIFT FOR _____ COST _____ U.S. $ _____

ITEM _____

WHERE BOUGHT _____

GIFT FOR _____ COST _____ U.S. $ _____

ITEM _____

WHERE BOUGHT _____

GIFT FOR _____ COST _____ U.S. $ _____

ITEM _____

WHERE BOUGHT _____

GIFT FOR _____ COST _____ U.S. $ _____

ITEM _____

WHERE BOUGHT _____

GIFT FOR _____ COST _____ U.S. $ _____

PURCHASES

ITEM _____

WHERE BOUGHT _____

GIFT FOR _____ COST _____ U.S.$ _____

ITEM _____

WHERE BOUGHT _____

GIFT FOR _____ COST _____ U.S.$ _____

ITEM _____

WHERE BOUGHT _____

GIFT FOR _____ COST _____ U.S.$ _____

ITEM _____

WHERE BOUGHT _____

GIFT FOR _____ COST _____ U.S.$ _____

ITEM _____

WHERE BOUGHT _____

GIFT FOR _____ COST _____ U.S.$ _____

ADDRESSES

NAME _____

ADDRESS _____

_____ PHONE _____

NAME _____

ADDRESS _____

_____ PHONE _____

NAME _____

ADDRESS _____

_____ PHONE _____

NAME _____

ADDRESS _____

_____ PHONE _____

NAME _____

ADDRESS _____

_____ PHONE _____

ADDRESSES

NAME _____

ADDRESS _____

_____ PHONE_____

NAME _____

ADDRESS _____

_____ PHONE_____

NAME _____

ADDRESS _____

_____ PHONE_____

NAME _____

ADDRESS _____

_____ PHONE_____

NAME _____

ADDRESS _____

_____ PHONE_____

TRAVEL DIARY

DATE_____

DATE_____

DATE_____

DATE_____

DATE_____

DATE_____

DATE_____

TRAVEL DIARY

DATE_____

DATE_____

DATE_____

DATE_____

DATE_____

DATE_____

DATE_____